BECOMING A PEOPLE OF

Grace

FROM THE BIBLE-TEACHING MINISTRY OF

Charles R. SWINDOLL

INSIGHT FOR LIVING

Charles R. Swindoll graduated in 1963 from Dallas Theological Seminary, where he now serves as the school's fourth president, helping to prepare a new generation of men and women for the ministry. Chuck has served in pastorates in three states: Massachusetts, Texas, and California, including almost twenty-three years at the First Evangelical Free Church in Fullerton, California. He is currently senior pastor of Stonebriar Community Church in Frisco, Texas, north of Dallas. His sermon messages have been aired over radio since 1979 as the *Insight for Living* broadcast. A best-selling author, he has written numerous books and booklets on many subjects.

Based on the outlines and transcripts of Charles. R. Swindoll's sermons, the Bible study guide text was developed and written by the Pastoral Ministries Department of Insight for Living.

Editor in Chief:
Cynthia Swindoll

Study Guide Writer:
Jason Shepherd

Senior Editor and Assistant Writer:
Wendy Peterson

Assistant Editors:
Glenda Schlahta
Karene Wells

Editor:
Christianne Varvel

Rights and Permissions:
The Meredith Agency

Graphic System Administrator:
Bob Haskins

Director, Communications Division:
John Norton

Print Production Manager:
Don Bernstein

Print Buyer:
Becki Sue Gómez

Unless otherwise identified, all Scripture references are from the New American Standard Bible, © The Lockman Foundation 1960, 1962, 1963, 1968, 1971, 1972, 1973, 1975, 1977, 1995. Used by permission. Scripture taken from the Holy Bible, New International Version, Copyright © 1973, 1978, 1984 International Bible Society, used by permission of Zondervan Bible Publishers [NIV]. Other translations cited are the King James Version [KJV], the Living Bible [LB], the New English Bible [NEB], and The Message [THE MESSAGE].

Scripture quotations from THE MESSAGE. Copyright © by Eugene H. Peterson 1993, 1994, 1995. Used by permission of NavPress Publishing Group.

An effort has been made to locate sources and obtain permission where necessary for the quotations used in this book. In the event of any unintentional omission, a modification will gladly be incorporated in future printings.

ISBN 1-57972-366-7
Cover design: Lauriana Fortuna
Cover image: © 2001 (Sandra Baker)/Stone; © 2001/Hulton Getty
Printed in the United States of America

CONTENTS

INTRODUCTION

Have you ever received a letter so good that you wanted to frame it? What made it so special? Why would you want to look at it every day and display it to all who entered your house?

Just off the top of my head, I can think of two reasons. First, the letter might have come from an important person, maybe a military leader or a government official—maybe even the president or prime minister of your country. Second, it might contain a special message. Your mother's last letter to you before she passed away might be worth framing. Or your dad's words of wisdom on your eighteenth birthday.

Paul's letter to the Ephesians is a "framer." It not only comes from the most important Person—God (who inspired Paul)—but it also contains a very special and unique message. Unlike some of the apostle's other letters, it wasn't written to rebuke heresy or solve problems. Paul's hands were totally free to write from his heart, so he wrote about our new position in Christ and our new practice in His body. Paul extolled God's grace and encouraged us to be people that exemplify that grace. In short, he penned one of the most majestic, powerful letters in the New Testament!

Join me, won't you, in this study of Ephesians? You won't regret opening yourself up to its dynamic message. This letter will change your life; I guarantee it. So turn the page, and let's get started!

Charles R. Swindoll

PUTTING TRUTH INTO ACTION

Knowledge apart from application falls short of God's desire for His children. He wants us to apply what we learn so that we will change and grow. This Bible study guide was prepared with these goals in mind. As you go through the following pages, we hope your desire to discover biblical truth will grow as your understanding of God's Word increases and that you will be encouraged to apply what you've learned.

To assist you in your study, we've included a section called ❧ **Living Insights** at the end of each lesson. These exercises will challenge you to study further and to think of specific ways to put your discoveries into action.

On occasion a lesson is followed by a ◥ **Digging Deeper** section, which gives you additional information and resources to probe further into some issues raised in that lesson.

There are many ways to use this guide—in personal devotions, group studies, discussions with friends and family, and Sunday School classes. And, of course, it's an ideal study aid when you're listening to its corresponding *Insight for Living* radio series.

To benefit most from this Bible study guide, we would encourage you to consider it a spiritual journal. That's why we've included space in the **Living Insights** for recording your thoughts and discoveries. We hope you'll return to those sections often for review and encouragement as you continue to grow in your walk with Christ.

Insight for Living

BECOMING A PEOPLE OF

Chapter 1

EPHESIANS:
A LIFE-CHANGING LETTER

An Overview of Ephesians

Have you ever thought of Paul as a spiritual warrior? Just a glance at his New Testament letters reveals that he spent most of his time fighting one thing or another—debunking heresies, challenging enemies of the faith, expelling ignorance, and shaking Christians from apathy and laziness.

In his Corinthian letters, for example, he confronted quarrels that were tearing apart the church. In Galatians, he battled legalists who were trying to imprison the souls of the believers. He also fought confusion and fear (2 Thess.), lack of confidence (1 and 2 Tim.), and false doctrine (Col.). It seems as though Paul was always battling something.

But what would the apostle have written if he hadn't had any heresies to correct, any fights to referee, or any false teachers to expose? The answer is Ephesians. In this grand epistle, Paul exchanged his sword for a paintbrush. He stepped out of his military gear, away from all the conflicts in his world, to paint a magnificent portrait of Christ and His people. Why? Commentator Walter Liefeld states the letter's purpose:

> Paul wrote to expand the horizons of his readers, so that they might understand better the dimensions of God's eternal purpose and grace and come to appreciate the high goals God has for the church.[1]

---

1. Walter L. Liefeld, introduction to Ephesians, in *The NIV Study Bible*, gen. ed. Kenneth L. Barker (Grand Rapids, Mich.: Zondervan Bible Publishers, 1985), p. 1790.

In Ephesians, Paul lifted his head above the dust and smoke of strife to give us a view of what Christ did for us and why. His letter provides us with a higher perspective—a new vision of our purpose and calling as the body of Christ and how we are to live it out. It blends some of the loftiest theology in Scripture with some of the most practical teaching. It shows us the deeper reality of God's all-encompassing rule and how our daily, seemingly mundane lives contribute to the accomplishment of His glorious plan.

Before we work our way through Ephesians verse by verse, learning all the nuances of Christ's majesty and His design for the church, let's explore the background of this letter and see how Paul put it together.

The World in Which the Letter Was Written

Paul may not have had any specific problems to address within the church's walls at that time, but outside, his world was filled with violence. In fact, he and the Ephesian church lived in a society that was lethal to Christians.

Roman Persecution

When Paul was writing, Nero ruled the Roman Empire. More than any other Caesar, this maniacal emperor persecuted Christians with sadistic glee. He blamed them for the infamous fire that nearly destroyed Rome—a fire he probably set himself—and used it as an excuse to brutally murder many of them. Even the ancient historian Tacitus, who also hated Christians, admitted that Nero took his tortures to the extreme:

> First, Nero had self-acknowledged Christians arrested. Then, on their information, large numbers of others were condemned—not so much for incendiarism as for their anti-social tendencies. Their deaths were made farcical. Dressed in wild animals' skins, they were torn to pieces by dogs, or crucified, or made into torches to be ignited after dark as substitutes for daylight. Nero provided his Gardens for the spectacle, and exhibited displays in the Circus [Maximus]. . . . It was felt that they were being sacrificed to one man's brutality rather than to the national interest.[2]

2. Tacitus, *The Annals of Imperial Rome*, rev. ed., trans. Michael Grant (1977; reprint, New York, N.Y.: Penguin Classics, 1988), pp. 365–66.

Many in Rome, though perhaps unwilling to go to the extremes that Nero did, believed that Christians were criminals deserving "ruthless punishment."[3] So the Ephesian believers needed to stay sharp, on their toes, always ready to give a defense of their faith . . . and ready to die for it too.

In spite of such wicked persecution, Paul challenged the Ephesians to think beyond mere survival. His letter instructed them to live and experience every subtlety of the Christian life—to operate as a fully functioning church.

Why give this particular message at this particular time? Wouldn't they be too busy avoiding Nero's henchmen to think about anything else? Paul obviously thought otherwise. To him, worshiping Christ and participating in His plan were not to be done in good times only. If they had to face the earthly terrors of crucifixion or being burned to death, they had to believe that their faith was worth it. They had to know the heavenly triumph in their earthly defeat.

Ephesian Paganism

In addition to the empire's widespread persecution, the Ephesian believers faced a unique challenge. Ephesus was renowned for its paganism, and the temple of the Greek goddess Artemis stood as its crown jewel:[4]

> [The temple] was one of the seven wonders of the world. One of its features was its pillars. It contained one hundred and twenty-seven pillars, every one of them the gift of a king. All were made of marble, and some were studded with jewels and overlaid with gold.[5]

This temple cast a long shadow over the city. Not only did it control the town's mind-set, but it also drove its economy—a fact Paul discovered the hard way.

After he had taught that a god made by human hands was no god at all, a silversmith named Demetrius, who made shrines for

---

3. Tacitus, The Annals of Imperial Rome, p. 366.

4. In Roman mythology, Artemis was known as Diana.

5. William Barclay, The Letters to Timothy, Titus, and Philemon, rev. ed., The Daily Study Bible Series (Philadelphia, Pa.: Westminster Press, 1975), p. 89.

the temple, gathered his fellow tradesmen together to stir them into action. Paul would put them out of business with this teaching, Demetrius warned, but more than that, Paul would discredit their beloved goddess Artemis (Acts 19:23–27). His speech worked:

> When they heard this and were filled with rage, they began crying out, saying, "Great is Artemis of the Ephesians!" The city was filled with the confusion, and they rushed with one accord into the theater, dragging along Gaius and Aristarchus, Paul's traveling companions from Macedonia. And when Paul wanted to go into the assembly, the disciples would not let him. (vv. 28–30)

Paul probably would have been killed! From a Christian's perspective, Ephesus was a hostile environment, to say the least. Paul had experienced it personally, yet he still encouraged the believers there to do more than just "hang in there." He exhorted them to *walk*—to live openly—according to their calling (Eph. 4:1).

The Formation of the Ephesian Church

In the midst of this hostility, how was the Ephesian church formed in the first place? To answer this question, we need to go back in time to Paul's second missionary journey.

On that trip, he met two tentmakers, Priscilla and Aquila, while passing through Corinth. He soon became their friend and business partner and stayed with them for a while, making tents and teaching in the local synagogue (Acts 18:1–17). They traveled with him to Ephesus, where he left them and journeyed on to Caesarea and Antioch (vv. 18–22).

On his third missionary journey, Paul returned to Ephesus and found a group of disciples there, possibly members of Priscilla and Aquila's house church. The apostle baptized the converts and stayed in the city again, teaching first in the synagogue and later at a local school (19:1–9). In all, Paul's second visit to Ephesus lasted two years (v. 10), during which many miracles took place and the gospel spread like a wildfire (vv. 11–20).

Why did the Ephesian church continue to grow despite the anti-Christian nature of its city? Perhaps because of the amount of time Paul invested in it. He spent almost three years with the believers there—more than he had with any other local church.

The Holy Spirit used Paul's intimate knowledge of the Ephesians to write the specific message contained in his letter to them. He penned it while under house arrest in Rome, waiting to appear before Caesar.[6]

The Structure of the Letter

Ephesians has two parts with two themes. Chapters 1–3 show that Christ, through His death, Resurrection, and exaltation, has reconciled us to God and united Jews and Gentiles into "one body" (2:16), of which Jesus is the Head. This section is *doctrinal*, revealing our position in Christ. Chapters 4–6 instruct us on how to live in light of our position—our new identity in Christ. This section is *practical*, explaining our part in accomplishing God's work.

Both parts have three chapters and three subsections. Three prayers also reinforce this structural balance: Paul prayed for the Ephesians' enlightenment at the beginning (chap. 1), for their ability to grasp Christ's love in the middle (chap. 3), and asked for their prayers for him at the end of the letter (chap. 6). Paul also fashioned a triad of sevens: seven spiritual blessings in Christ (chap. 1), seven unities of the body of Christ (chap. 4), and seven pieces of armor for use in spiritual battles (chap. 6).

Chapter 1 reveals what God has done for us and emphasizes God's generosity and Christ's headship. Verse 3 beautifully reveals the first theme:

> Blessed be the God and Father of our Lord Jesus Christ, who has blessed us with every spiritual blessing in the heavenly places in Christ.

And verses 20–23 reveal the grandeur of the second theme:

> [God] raised [Christ] from the dead and seated Him at His right hand in the heavenly places, far above all rule and authority and power and dominion, and every name that is named, not only in this age but also in the one to come. And He put all things in subjection under His feet, and gave Him as head

6. Some scholars believe that the letter to the Ephesians may have been a "cyclical" letter— a letter that Paul wanted passed from church to church—and not written solely to the congregation at Ephesus. These scholars suggest that it may be the letter referred to in Colossians 4:16. The evidence for this position, however, is inconclusive. It's possible, but not certain.

over all things to the church, which is His body, the fullness of Him who fills all in all.

Chapter 2 turns to discuss what Christ has done in us and focuses on God's grace:

But God, being rich in mercy, because of His great love with which He loved us, even when we were dead in our transgressions, made us alive together with Christ (by grace you have been saved), and raised us up with Him, and seated us with Him in the heavenly places in Christ Jesus. (vv. 4–6)

It also exults in His reconciliation of all people to each other:

For He Himself is our peace, who made both groups [Jews and Gentiles] into one and broke down the barrier of the dividing wall. (v. 14)

Chapter 3 emphasizes revelation, discussing what the mystery means to us:

That by revelation there was made known to me the mystery, as I wrote before in brief. By referring to this, when you read you can understand my insight into the mystery of Christ, which in other generations was not made known to the sons of men, as it has now been revealed to His holy apostles and prophets in the Spirit. (vv. 3–5)

Chapter 4 shifts from the firm footing of doctrine to the practical steps of faith. Paul moved from description to direction: "I, the prisoner of the Lord, implore you to walk in a manner worthy of the calling with which you have been called" (v. 1). Chapter 4, then, explains the walk of the believer. Our steps include:

✔ humility	✔ maturity
✔ gentleness	✔ stability
✔ patience	✔ honesty
✔ unity	✔ harmony
✔ tolerance	✔ kindness
✔ love	✔ compassion
✔ knowledge	✔ forgiveness

The next section, the life of the imitator (5:1–6:9), shows how emulators of Christ conduct themselves in three distinct spheres:

1. In the world

2. In the home

3. In the workplace

Paul concluded his instructions by explaining the strategy of the warrior (6:10–20). This strategy includes a plan of attack against both demonic forces and human opposition.

In his final thoughts, Paul ended the letter just as he began it—with grace and peace (6:21–24).

Three Thoughts to Remember

As we study this important letter, let's keep three thoughts in mind:

- A *reminder—we are all under the headship of Christ as Lord.* Because we serve Jesus and answer to Him, we're to be *submissive,* both to Him and to each other.

- A *relief—we belong to a body.* We're not alone; we don't have to act on our own or handle our problems by ourselves. We can take refuge in the body of Christ. As a necessary prerequisite, we need to be *committed* to Christ and to each other.

- A *reassurance—we can stand against the assault of our enemies.* We have God's resources available to us. To take advantage of them, we need to become *equipped* to utilize them properly.

Want to have a fuller sense of reassurance and relief about your life as a Christian? Join us in this study of Ephesians—it will show you how to become fully submissive, committed, and equipped, allowing you to better worship Christ and participate in His plan for your life.

🌿 *Living Insights*

Most of us are probably as busy as Paul—so busy that we rarely have time to sit back, relax, and just think. We may not have heretics to fight, false teachers to expose, or sadistic Roman emperors to run from, but that doesn't mean we have any more time on our hands. Our high tech, information-age society has forced us to live in the fastest-paced culture the world has ever seen.

But the benefits of taking time out can be nothing short of miraculous. Just ask Paul, who took time to contemplate God's gift of Christ and everything we have because of Him. So let's follow his lead by turning aside from the immediate pressures of life to soak up the timeless truths found in Ephesians. Read through the entire letter in one sitting; then reflect on the following questions to prepare for your study of this rich book.

It's no mistake that Paul describes our *position* in Christ before he exhorts us to *practice* the Christian life. What does this tell you about the nature of change? Which comes first, belief or behavior? Can you find any other Bible verses to support your answer?

_____

_____

_____

_____

Paul gave a lot of attention to Christ, especially His importance and power. What does this tell you about the source of change? Should Christians seek to change themselves, or do they have a deeper source of power from which to draw? Can you think of any examples from Paul's life?

_____

_____

_____

Based on what Paul said in the letter, what should we be most concerned about in our churches today? Programs? Numerical growth? Church marketing? Name some of the topics Paul addressed.

_____

_____

_____

_____

What do you hope this study of Ephesians will teach you about your own walk with God?

_____

_____

_____

How would you like this study to change you? Your church involvement? Family life? Friendships?

_____

_____

_____

Now that you have a grasp of the letter and some goals in mind for your study of it, prepare yourself even more by committing to read Ephesians in a single sitting every day for the rest of the week. When you finish the study, you'll see that the time spent will be well worth it!

OUR NEW

Position

IN CHRIST

Chapter 2

UNLOADING THE
THEOLOGICAL TRUCK

Ephesians 1:1–2

Sir Francis Bacon once wrote,

> Some books are to be tasted, others to be swallowed,
> and some few to be chewed and digested.[1]

The books of Scripture are certainly among the few worthy of being absorbed into our minds and hearts. They lie on a separate, distinct plane above all others. Not only are they wholly accurate and infallible, but they also come from the very mouth of God—they contain *His* words, not just those of the human authors who penned them (see 2 Tim. 3:16).[2] As such, God designed the Scriptures to nourish us and to penetrate every cell of our souls. He wants the words to fill us and become part of our deepest being.

The book of Ephesians is no exception. To make sure that we absorb every spiritual nutrient this book has to offer, let's delve into a little more background before entering our verse-by-verse study.

The Author

Liberal scholars question Paul's authorship of this letter because, unlike his other writings, it does not address any local, personal concerns relating to the church at Ephesus. However, the methodical and flowing development of his themes certainly mark the letter as his, and his own introduction should dispel any doubts:

> Paul, an apostle of Christ Jesus by the will of God.
> (Eph. 1:1a)

What made Paul's style so unique and recognizable? A look at his background will help us understand what made Paul, Paul.

---

1. Sir Francis Bacon, as quoted in *Bartlett's Familiar Quotations*, 15th ed., rev. and enl., ed. Emily Morison Beck (Boston, Mass.: Little, Brown and Co., 1980), p. 181.

2. Scripture is *inspired*, which means God directed the human authors' thoughts to write what was on His mind. The inspiration of the Bible is *verbal*, which means the words that were chosen by the human authors are the exact ones God desired.

Paul's Background

Although the Bible doesn't tell us much about Paul's life directly, we can, with some research, draw some conclusions about his life.

To begin with, we do know that Paul was a Jew from Tarsus, a significant city in the province of Cilicia (Acts 9:11; 21:39; 22:3). Pauline biographer John Pollock tells us that Tarsus "was the principle city of the lush plain of Cilicia in the southwest corner of Asia Minor" and that it "was a fusion of civilizations at peace under the rule of Rome," which included indigenous Cilicians, Hittites, "light-skinned" Greeks, Assyrians, Persians, and Macedonians.[3]

So Paul grew up in a multicultural world, not too dissimilar from today's Western societies. He was apparently reared in a stable home, and his father was possibly a wealthy tentmaker.[4] Acts 23:16 tells us he had at least one sibling, a sister, but nothing is known of his mother.

We also can surmise that Paul grew up among strong religious convictions. His parents had him circumcised on the eighth day, in strict accordance with the Law (Phil. 3:5; Lev. 12:3). As an adolescent, he was trained in the Law under Gamaliel, "the most honored rabbi of the first century,"[5] where he

> learned to dissect a text until scores of possible meanings were disclosed according to the considered opinion of generations of rabbis. . . . Paul learned to debate in the question-and-answer style known to the ancient world as the "diatribe," and to expound, for a rabbi was not only part preacher but part lawyer, who prosecuted or defended those who broke the sacred Law.[6]

---

3. John Pollock, *The Apostle: A Life of Paul* (Wheaton, Ill.: Scripture Press Publications, Victor Books, 1985), pp. 14–15.

4. Pollock, *The Apostle*, pp. 15–16. We know Paul's family was wealthy because he was born a Roman citizen (Acts 22:25–28), a privilege given only for distinguished civil service or for a substantial fee. Perhaps Paul's grandfather had helped General Pompey gain Cilicia for Rome or had aided the great statesman and orator Cicero as he governed Cilicia, or maybe Paul's father had tendered a large donation to the governing officials. In any case, only a man of wealth would be able to do so.

5. Lewis Foster, note on Acts 22:3, in *The NIV Study Bible*, gen. ed. Kenneth L. Barker (Grand Rapids, Mich.: Zondervan Bible Publishers, 1985), p. 1689.

6. Pollock, *The Apostle*, pp. 17–18.

How did Paul fare in this phase of his training? By his own admission, he "was advancing in Judaism beyond many of my contemporaries among my countrymen, being more extremely zealous for my ancestral traditions" (Gal. 1:14). Pollock adds that Paul was well on his way to taking a seat on the Sanhedrin in the Hall of Polished Stones to become a "ruler of the Jews."[7]

Brilliant of mind, strong in character, solid in leadership—Paul developed these qualities in his youth and carried them with him through his conversion, missionary ministry, and, ultimately, his writing. Remembering what kind of man Paul was sheds a bright light on the content of his letter to the Ephesians. Who he was influenced what he wrote.[8]

Paul, "an Apostle"

Not only was the letter to the Ephesians impacted by Paul's unique character, but it was also supported by the special office he held: he was an *apostle* (1:1a). The Greek term, *apostolos*, simply means "sent one,"[9] but the term as Paul used it has a specialized meaning. It describes men who were handpicked by God for a special purpose:

> Out of Jesus' many disciples, He selected twelve to be His apostles. These were the men who were sent by Jesus to take His message to the world and then raise up churches. Paul also became an apostle by the appointment of the risen Christ, who encountered Paul on the road to Damascus (see Acts 9).[10]

In Jesus' physical absence, these men became the foundation of the church—second only to Christ Himself (Eph. 2:20). When reading Ephesians, it's important to remember that this letter came from

---

7. Pollock, *The Apostle*, p. 18.

8. Although the words chosen by the human authors are the exact ones desired by God, God did not dictate to them. Rather, He shaped the authors over the courses of their lives, allowing them to contribute their own unique educations, personalities, experiences, and vocabularies to the writing process to produce documents that were fully divine *and* fully human. Consequently, knowledge of the human author can help us understand the text more accurately.

9. "Apostle," in WordFocus in 2 Corinthians 11, in *The Nelson Study Bible*, gen. ed. Earl D. Radmacher (Nashville, Tenn.: Thomas Nelson, 1997), p. 1962.

10. "Apostle," in *The Nelson Study Bible*, p. 1962.

an apostle of Christ. Paul constantly asserted and defended his position, especially in 2 Corinthians, so that his readers would fully appreciate the authority and authenticity of his instructions. John R. W. Stott notes:

> For we must regard its author neither as a private individual who is ventilating his personal opinions, nor as a gifted but fallible human teacher, nor even as the church's greatest missionary hero, but as "an apostle of Christ Jesus by the will of God," and therefore as a teacher whose authority is precisely the authority of Jesus Christ himself, in whose name and by whose inspiration he writes.[11]

The Recipients

Paul wrote his letter to the believers in Ephesus:

> To the saints who are at Ephesus and who are faithful in Christ Jesus. (Eph. 1:1b)

This fact seems simple enough, but let's not skim past it too quickly. Paul used significant terms to describe these people.

"Saints"

He first identified the Ephesian believers as "saints." When we think of saints, we conjure up images of statues in cathedrals, stained glass, miraculous apparitions, and mystical encounters. Paul had none of this in mind. To him, a saint was anyone who believed in Christ—anyone who had been chosen by God and set apart for Him. James Montgomery Boice helps us understand what is involved in being a saint:

> Every Christian is a saint, and every saint is a Christian. Moreover, every true Christian is in some sense separated from the world. It does not mean that we are taken out of the world. That is not the way God operates. But it does mean that we are removed from it in the sense of not really belonging to the world any longer. If we are truly Christ's, we

11. John R. W. Stott, *The Message of Ephesians: God's New Society*, The Bible Speaks Today Series (Downers Grove, Ill.: InterVarsity Press, 1979), pp. 21–22. Used by permission of InterVarsity Press-US and InterVarsity Press-UK.

have a new nature, a new set of loyalties, and a new agenda. We belong to a different kingdom.[12]

So Paul directed his words to the saints in Ephesus—to those who, like him, had been set apart to serve God. Ephesians was an "in-house" letter to members of God's family, teaching the Father's wisdom in order that they might grow. Since we, too, are saints, we've been set apart to learn God's ways and grow in Him as well.

"Faithful in Christ Jesus"

These believers, Paul stated, were also "faithful in Christ Jesus"—a fidelity that should not be taken lightly, since many of the other churches to whom Paul wrote, particularly the Corinthians and Galatians, weren't quite so truehearted.

Faithful, in the New Testament, can mean "exercising faith" (having expressed faith) or "to continue in faith" (to keep the faith).[13] In Ephesians 1:1, it probably means both. The Ephesians believed in Christ for the forgiveness of their sins and were continuing to rely on God and grow in Him.

Notice that Paul focused on their faithfulness "in Christ." This, and the equivalent "in Him," is one of the most important phrases in the whole book of Ephesians. Paul, in all his letters, used these phrases more than fifty times. In the first fourteen verses of Ephesians 1 alone, he repeated them almost a dozen times.

Despite this phrase's wide usage, however, it remains one of the least understood concepts in the New Testament. Like "saints," "in Christ" describes all believers. Through faith, each one of us is in Christ. But the phrase does more than state the fact of our salvation. It points to our "being *joined to Christ* in one spiritual body so that what is true of him is also true for us"[14] (emphasis added). John Stott further expands on what it means to be joined to Christ:

> To be "in Christ" is to be personally and vitally united to Christ, as branches are to the vine and members to the body, and thereby also to Christ's people. For it is impossible to be part of the Body

12. James Montgomery Boice, *Ephesians: An Expositional Commentary* (Grand Rapids, Mich.: Baker Books, 1997), p. 5. Used by permission.

13. Boice, *Ephesians*, pp. 5–6. Used by permission.

14. Boice, *Ephesians*, p. 6. Used by permission.

without being related to both the Head and the members. Much of what the epistle later develops is already here in bud. According to the New Testament—and especially Paul—to be a Christian is in essence to be "in Christ," one with him and with his people.[15]

So, to be in Christ means to be joined not only to our Lord but also to our brothers and sisters in the faith. And this makes sense because in order to remain faithful to Christ, we need the support of His people—and they need ours. The Ephesians obviously had clung to each other and remained true to their Savior, and Paul commended them for it.

The Author's Greeting to the Recipients

After identifying himself and his audience, Paul extended his greeting:

> Grace to you and peace from God our Father and the Lord Jesus Christ. (1:2)

Grace and peace—that's where the apostle began. *Grace* means God's undeserved favor. It is "the free, unmerited, unexpected love of God, and all the benefits, delights, and comforts which flow from it. It means that while we were sinners and enemies we have been treated as sons and heirs."[16]

Peace is one of the products of grace. When we've been blessed by God's undeserved gift of salvation, we have been reconciled to God—we have peace, both *with* God and *in* ourselves. God's wrath no longer burns against us (see Rom. 5:1, 9; Col. 1:20), and we, as a result, no longer have anything to fear. Peace, then, produces a joy that transcends circumstances and all boundaries between fellow believers—whether it be race, class, gender, intellect, or anything else.

Paul included grace and peace in all of his greetings. He wanted all of his readers to experience God's unmerited love and rest in their daily living. And the Lord wants that for us too.

---

15. Stott, *The Message of Ephesians*, pp. 22–23. Used by permission of InterVarsity Press-US and InterVarsity Press-UK.

16. R. P. C. Hanson, as quoted by Bruce B. Barton, Philip Comfort, Kent Keller, Linda K. Taylor, and Dave Veerman in *Ephesians*, Life Application Bible Commentary Series (Wheaton, Ill.: Tyndale House Publishers, Inc., 1996), p. 7.

Let's dig into this wonderful book a little further, briefly outlining some of the treasures that lie just ahead.

The Outline

Paul unloaded a truckload of theological truths in just the first chapter, which has basically two sections: in verses 3–14, *Paul praises God* for what He's done for us in Christ; in verses 15–23, *Paul prays for his readers* to know Christ better.

The focus of Paul's heart, even though he was in prison, was on Christ and His followers. He exalted God for the riches He has given us in Christ, and he wanted his readers to exult in the hope that God has given to all who take Jesus as their Savior. How could Paul's spirit soar like this while his body was in shackles? Christ had control of his mind, his heart, his attitude, his desires, his motivation, and his perspective. Of course, Paul wasn't perfect, as he told the Philippians:

> Not that I have already . . . become perfect, but
> I press on so that I may lay hold of that for which
> also I was laid hold of by Christ Jesus. (Phil. 3:12)

But Christ was at the center of Paul's life and thoughts, as the first part of Ephesians 1 shows. We'll study the theological truths Paul set out in verses 3–14 in our next chapter, but here is a preview of all that God has done for us through Christ:

- God "has blessed us with every spiritual blessing" (v. 3).

- God has chosen us in Christ "before the foundation of the world" (v. 4).

- God has "predestined us to adoption as sons through Jesus Christ" (v. 5).

- God has secured our "redemption through [Christ's] blood" (v. 7a).

- God has forgiven us "of our trespasses" (v. 7b).

- God has lavished His grace on us (vv. 7b–8).

- God has "made known to us the mystery of His will" (v. 9).

- God has provided us with an inheritance (v. 11).

- God has "sealed" us in Christ (v. 13).

- God has given the Holy Spirit "as a pledge of our inheritance" (vv. 13b–14).

Notice that none of these points begin with "We have"—all of them originate with God and are a gift from Him. We can't gain a single one of these blessings with our own efforts; we're absolutely dependent on God's grace—which is why He alone should get the glory:

> To the praise of the glory of His grace, which He freely bestowed on us. . . . To the end that we who were the first to hope in Christ would be to the praise of His glory. . . . With a view to the redemption of God's own possession, to the praise of His glory. (vv. 6, 12, 14)

There's so much grace and glory that God wants to impart to us through Paul's letter. Let's take hold of His message—and let His message take hold of us!

✎ Living Insights

A single principle revolved around all of Paul's teachings about the Christian life. What was it? *Grace*. The apostle not only began his letters with a wish for his readers to have it, but he also ended his letters by imparting it. According to Paul, grace is not only the basis of our salvation, but it is also the means by which we live the Christian life.

Living by grace means accepting ourselves and others—failures and all. It means forgiving and going on. It means refusing to incarcerate ourselves in a cage of guilt or put others there.

A verse-by-verse study of Ephesians will transform your life by helping you learn how to live by grace. Take a few minutes to reflect on your life so as to maximize the time you spend in this book.

Have you had some spiritual failures recently, like losing your temper, succumbing to lust, or fudging on the facts you give your boss? What have they been?

_____

_____

How do you imagine God reacts to these failures? Is He angrily stomping and shouting, woefully disappointed and disapproving, or graciously understanding and compassionate?

_____

_____

_____

How do you feel about yourself when you fail?

_____

_____

_____

How do you respond to others when they fail?

_____

_____

_____

If you find that you're not living in grace already, begin right now. Place your trust in Christ, who died for your sins—*all of them*. And forgive the people who have sinned against you; after all, Christ died for them too. Feel the peace coming? It's on the way!

Chapter 3

TEN REASONS TO GIVE GOD PRAISE
Ephesians 1:3–14

One of the most stirring moments in American military history came not on the field of battle but in a chapel, during the funeral service of Robert E. Lee—a Confederate general, American hero, and man of God.

Unfortunately, a local flood prevented many of Lee's famous officers from attending the service. But the bad weather could not keep away the men Lee thought most honorable—the unknown privates of the infantry, many of whom came down from the mountains and coves of Virginia to pay their last respects. Biographer J. Steven Wilkins describes what happened in the chapel that day:

> These were men of few words but solid convictions. They had been silent as they passed by his body. They had been reserved in the display of their emotions as they participated in the ceremonies of the day, but no one felt more deeply than they the realities of life and death. When the final committal had been read by Reverend Pendleton, the gathered congregation began to sing *How Firm a Foundation*, the famous hymn General Lee had loved so much in his lifetime.
>
> Once again, the familiar sound of the singing of the Army of Northern Virginia rang across the valley. The men who had sung so many times with their general gave him his last tribute by singing at the top of their voices the praises of God and of the great salvation. The old hymn echoed off the buildings of the town, and the surrounding mountains themselves rang with the beautiful melody. It was perhaps the most fitting epitaph of all.[1]

---

1. J. Steven Wilkins, *Call of Duty: The Sterling Nobility of Robert E. Lee* (Nashville, Tenn.: Highland Books, Cumberland House Publishing, 1997), pp. 178–179.

Through song, these men delivered a personal eulogy to their departed general. *Webster's* tells us that "eulogy" means "high praise."[2] The term is actually a transliteration of an ancient Greek word, *eulogia,* meaning "praise," "fine speaking," or "blessing."[3]

A Eulogy to God

Paul, continuing his letter to the Ephesians, overwhelmingly praised God by using *eulogia* three times in a single verse:

> *Blessed* be the God and Father of our Lord Jesus Christ, who has *blessed* us with every spiritual *blessing* in the heavenly places in Christ. (1:3, emphasis added)

With the loving dedication of a loyal soldier, Paul praised his General, "the God and Father of our Lord Jesus Christ." This effusion of praise comes after a fairly sedate introduction by the apostle (see vv. 1–2).

Why this sudden paean of praise? Paul himself gave the answer. In fact, he gave ten answers—ten blessings with which God has blessed us. These favors, listed in the next eleven verses, are not for the apostle only, but for us as well. Let's take a look at each one so that we, too, can experience the heights and depths of Paul's adoration of God.

Ten Reasons to Give God Praise

In verses 3–14, Paul put God's blessings on display. And behind the scenes lies an important theological truth—the Trinity. Take note of each Member:

- vv. 3–6: the *Father initiated* His plan of salvation,

- vv. 7–12: the *Son implemented* the plan,

- vv. 13–14: the *Spirit empowers* the plan.

Let's look at Paul's ten answers to the question, "Why praise God?"

---

2. *Merriam-Webster's Collegiate Dictionary,* 10th ed., see "eulogy."

3. Walter Bauer, *A Greek-English Lexicon of the New Testament and Other Early Christian Literature,* 2d ed. Revised and augmented by F. Wilbur Gingrich and Frederick W. Danker, from Walter Bauer's 5th ed., 1958 (Chicago, Ill.: University of Chicago Press, 1979), p. 322.

1. Because He Blessed Us with Every Spiritual Blessing

Verses 3–6 transport us to eternity past—before light, matter, or even time existed. Yet God was there, making decisions that would impact the course of history. The first of God's decisions that Paul mentioned is His decision to "[bless] us with every spiritual blessing" (v. 3).

"Blessing" means "to benefit, to prosper, to give contentment."[4] The verb occurs hundreds of times in the Old Testament, revealing that God enjoys blessing His people. Here Paul used the past tense, "has blessed," indicating that this prospering of believers has already taken place.

What kind of blessings does God offer? Paul referred to the "heavenly places" (v. 3), which means the blessings were secured in heaven and then given to us. They came from above. In other words, they're heavenly, not earthly; spiritual, not material—eternal, not temporal.

2. Because He Has Chosen Us

> Just as He chose us in Him before the foundation of the world, that we would be holy and blameless before Him. (v. 4)

Entire books have been written on this verse because it does more than describe a blessing; it forms the basis for a whole doctrine.

> That God *chose us* forms the basis of the doctrine of election—defined as God's choice of an individual or group for a specific purpose or destiny. The doctrine of election teaches that we are saved only because of God's grace and mercy; as believers we are not saved by our own merit. It focuses on God's purpose or will (1:5, 9, 11), not on ours. God does not save us because we deserve it but because he graciously and freely gives salvation. We did not influence God's decision to save us; he saved us according to his plan. Thus, we may not take credit for our salvation or take pride in our wise choice.[5]

4. Bruce B. Barton, Philip Comfort, Kent Keller, Linda K. Taylor, and Dave Veerman, *Ephesians*, Life Application Bible Commentary Series (Wheaton, Ill.: Tyndale House Publishers, 1996), p. 8.

5. Barton and others, *Ephesians*, p. 11.

This profound truth was designed to motivate us to "walk in a manner worthy of the calling with which you have been called" (4:1). Our response to election should be like Queen Victoria's reaction when she realized she would one day be queen:

> When she was young, Victoria was shielded from the fact that she would be the next ruling monarch of England lest this knowledge spoil her. When her teacher finally did let her discover for herself that she would one day be Queen of England, Victoria's response was, "Then I will be good!" Her life would be controlled by her position. No matter where she was, Victoria was governed by the fact that she sat on the throne of England.[6]

Likewise, we should govern our actions by the joy of our election. Thoughts of God's choosing us should both motivate and humble us.

3. Because He Has Predestined and Adopted Us

God elected us so that He also could adopt us into His family:

> He predestined us to adoption as sons through Jesus Christ to Himself, according to the kind intention of His will. (1:5)

"Predestined," *proorisas* in the Greek, means "marked out beforehand."[7] Because God chose to elect us, He placed a special mark on us—He predestined us with the knowledge that He would one day adopt us.

Our relationship with God has been likened to one in which a judge condemns a lawbreaker and then comes out from behind the bench and pays the penalty. But God does more than that—He takes us home and adopts us into His family![8]

Under Roman law, which served as a backdrop for Paul's writing, adopted children enjoyed the same rights as natural children.[9] In

---

6. Warren Wiersbe, *Be Rich: Are You Losing the Things That Money Can't Buy?* (Colorado Springs, Colo.: Chariot Victor Books, 1976), pp. 13–14.

7. Barton and others, *Ephesians*, p. 14.

8. Barton and others, *Ephesians*, p. 14.

9. See John R. W. Stott, *The Message of Ephesians: God's New Society*, The Bible Speaks Today Series (Downer's Grove, Ill.: InterVarsity Press, 1979), p. 39.

the same way, we enjoy the same rights and privileges as Christ Himself—God's natural Son.

The doctrines of election and predestination seem to contradict another truth taught clearly in Scripture—that humans have been given the choice to believe in God or not, known as "free will." Many theologians have engaged themselves in the election/free will debate and have asserted a number of approaches to the issue. For believers who acknowledge that both concepts must be true, since both are taught in Scripture, the best way to understand the issue is to view election from God's viewpoint and free will from ours.

God knows the elect and the non-elect. We, on the other hand, desire to respond to the gospel and present it to everyone we meet.[10]

4. Because He Has Redeemed Us

> To the praise of the glory of His grace, which He freely bestowed on us in the Beloved. In Him we have redemption through His blood. (vv. 6–7a)

In verse 7, we see the second stage of Paul's presentation—Christ's implementation of God's plan. *Redemption* means *purchasing and setting free by paying a price.* In Old Testament times, the word referred to a person's being set free from slavery or prison (Lev. 25:47–54). Redeeming this person involved paying a price called a *ransom.* Since God also redeemed us—set us free from the shackles of sin— He had to pay a price. How did He do it? Not with silver or gold, but with the precious blood of His own Son (1 Pet. 1:18–19).

5. Because He Has Forgiven Us

> [We have] the forgiveness of our trespasses. (Eph. 1:7b)

Because Jesus paid our ransom, God no longer holds against us the debt our sin incurred. He has forgiven *all* our sins. This means that He no longer considers any of our transgressions—past, present, or future:

> As far as the east is from the west,
> So far has He removed our transgressions from us.
> (Ps. 103:12)

---

10. Some believe the doctrine of election is unjust because God, in choosing some for heaven, also chooses others for hell. This accusation is known as "double-predestination." Scripture does not teach that God predestines anyone to hell; the fact that He saves any of us is a function of His mercy.

6. Because He Lavished His Grace on Us

> According to the riches of His grace which He lavished on us. (Eph. 1:7c–8a)

God's grace is His unmerited favor. Unlike His mercy, which does *not* give us what we deserve, His grace gives us what we *don't* deserve. We deserve eternal damnation, but we receive infinite bliss. Why? Because of God's grace.

Paul used his characteristic word *riches* to ascribe value to this grace. We owe our lives, present and eternal, to the riches of God's grace. But this grace was not merely given, it was *lavished*—generously showered—on us. God wants to give grace to people—to us—and when He gives, He gives abundantly and extravagantly.[11]

7. Because He Made Known the Mystery of His Will

> In all wisdom and insight He made known to us the mystery of His will, according to His kind intention which He purposed in Him with a view to an administration suitable to the fullness of the times, that is, the summing up of all things in Christ, things in the heavens and things on the earth. (vv. 8b–10)

Although many of God's decisions were made in eternity past, He chose not to reveal some of them for a long time. Throughout the Old Testament times, Jews and Gentiles lived separate from each other. But through Jesus Christ, God made known His desire for all believers to integrate into a single body, the church. Paul described this plan of God's as a mystery, *musterion* in the Greek, which means it was a truth once hidden but now revealed.[12] Paul praised God for finally revealing His ultimate will.

8. Because He Has Provided an Eternal Inheritance

> In Him also we have obtained an inheritance, having been predestined according to His purpose who works all things after the counsel of His will, to the end that we who were the first to hope in Christ would be to the praise of His glory. (vv. 10b–12)

---

11. Barton and others, *Ephesians*, p. 20.

12. Harold W. Hoehner, "Ephesians," in *The Bible Knowledge Commentary*, New Testament edition, ed. John F. Walvoord and Roy B. Zuck (Colorado Springs, Colo.: Chariot Victor Publishing, 1983), p. 618.

The Greek term for "inheritance," *kleros*, generally refers to a lot or portion assigned to someone. Our inheritance takes two forms. In the present, we enjoy all the rewards of our salvation—peace with God and brotherhood with Christ. In the future, we'll inherit all the wealth of heaven. And our portion is irrevocable!

9. Because He Has Sealed Us in Christ

> In Him, you also, after listening to the message of truth, the gospel of your salvation—having also believed, you were sealed in Him with the Holy Spirit of promise. (v. 13)

Verse 13 ushers in the final phase of Paul's passage—the empowerment of God's plan through the Holy Spirit. By sealing us, God marked us as His own through the presence of the Holy Spirit in our lives: "In the ancient world, a seal was a form of identification used to authenticate and protect legal documents. A uniquely designed stone worn on a ring or necklace was used to mark clay or wax . . . on a document."[13] The sealing was a once-for-all act that gives us continued assurance that we're God's children, entitled to His riches and goodness.

10. Because He Has Guaranteed Our Inheritance

> Who is given as a pledge of our inheritance, with a view to the redemption of God's own possession, to the praise of His glory. (v. 14)

Pledge can also mean *deposit* or *guarantee*. In biblical times, the word was used to describe a down payment—a partial payment that promised that the buyer would complete the transaction and pay the full amount. The pledge was binding.[14]

In the same way, God's pledge of the Holy Spirit in our lives is the first payment of all the treasures that will be ours. We have the Spirit now but will experience Him even more fully when we live with Christ in heaven. God will keep all His promises to us; He will not renege on His pledge.[15]

---

13. Barton and others, *Ephesians*, p. 26.

14. Barton and others, *Ephesians*, p. 27.

15. Barton and others, *Ephesians*, p. 27.

Two Truths to Remember

We just walked through quite a list! As we consider each item, let's keep two thoughts in mind.

Since all ten blessings are implemented by Christ, they're all dependent on His Crucifixion and Resurrection. We must believe in Him to enter into His blessings. We must take that step of faith.

Since all ten blessings are initiated by God, they're all given to His glory. When talking about such wonderful benefits as these, it's easy to get sidetracked into thinking about ourselves and what we get out of the deal. Remember, it's all about God and glorifying Him.

Is your soul singing a eulogy to God yet? Maybe the hymn sung by the soldiers at General Lee's funeral mirror the sentiments of your own heart:

> The soul that on Jesus hath leaned for repose,
> I will not, I will not desert to his foes;
> That soul, tho all hell should endeavor to shake,
> I'll never—no, never—no, never forsake![16]

🕮 *Living Insights*

What better way to conclude a chapter on God's blessings than with a prayer of thanksgiving? Take the next few minutes to personalize the ten blessings listed below, describing how each one has manifested itself in your life. If nothing specific comes to mind, then write out what that blessing means to you and how it makes you feel.

He blessed you with every spiritual blessing: _____

_____

He chose you: _____

_____

He predestined and adopted you: _____

_____

16. "How Firm a Foundation" in *Great Hymns of the Faith*, comp. and ed. John W. Peterson (Grand Rapid, Mich.: Singspiration, Inc., Zondervan Publishing House, 1968), no. 268.

He redeemed you: _____

_____

He forgave you: _____

_____

He lavished His grace on you: _____

_____

He made known to you the mystery of His will: _____

_____

He provided you with an eternal inheritance: _____

_____

He sealed you in Christ: _____

_____

He guaranteed your inheritance: _____

_____

Feeling grateful to God? Spend time alone with Him right now, and thank Him for everything He's done for you.

 ## *Digging Deeper*

Sometimes touching on deep theological truths can create more questions than answers. We've covered some profound doctrines in this lesson, and two questions still linger. First, *why does God choose some and not others?* At a glance, this question appears innocent enough, but when we scrutinize it we find that it's based on a faulty premise. The question presupposes that humans have no guilt. It's as if we imagine God to be walking down the sidewalk and randomly picking whom He'll save from a group of innocent passers-by.

The sad fact is that we're all guilty of sin and deserving of eternal damnation. We should consider the extension of His grace to be as though He had walked into a prison's death row and mercifully pardoned some inmates to work for Him. Does God's pardoning of a few mean that the rest no longer deserve their sentence? Absolutely not! They're just as guilty as before, and it's ludicrous of them to accuse the pardoner of injustice. When contemplating this issue, the best question to ask is, "Why would God choose anyone at all?" The answer to *that* question, however, is one only God can provide.

Second, *how can we simultaneously embrace God's sovereignty and our responsibility?* Very few issues cause more confusion and arguments among Christians than the doctrines of election and free will. It's difficult to comprehend how the two coexist. But these were not theological concepts dreamed up by Paul; they appear throughout Scripture. Although we may not be able to reconcile them in our minds, we can admit that both are supported by Scripture and come with their own set of implications. Consider this:

Election . . .

- comes from the heart of God, not the mind of humans;
- inspires a desire to please God, not ignore Him;
- gives birth to gratitude, not complacency.

Free will . . .

- requires that we actively believe in Christ;
- focuses on living according to God's plan;
- requires that we witness for Christ by sharing the gospel.

God's truths—even the tough ones—were not designed to confuse or trouble us. Rather, they were intended to comfort, encourage, and motivate us. Understood correctly, they can do just that!

Chapter 4

PRAYING LIKE WE MEAN IT

Ephesians 1:15–19

The Christian ideal has not been tried and found wanting," G. K. Chesterton once said. "It has been found difficult; and left untried."[1] The same might be said of prayer.

Oh, we've all said our share of prayers . . . grace before meals, bedtime prayers, prayers in church services. But most of us are a little uncomfortable praying, a little unsure of how to go about it. We know that there is power in prayer, but that power sometimes seems a little beyond reach. We sincerely desire to connect with God, not just to repeat words from a book or intone meaningless clichés. We just don't know quite how to do it. And, truthfully, when it comes to praying in public . . . well, we'd be more comfortable with almost any other assignment!

Maybe that's because true prayer is so honest. It can't be done without vulnerability. Praying like we mean it means forgetting all the churchy-sounding phrases. It requires laying off the lingo and laying out our hearts before the Lord. More than likely, some of your best times of prayer have been in times of desperation—times when your need was too urgent for you to worry about things like what you were saying and how you were saying it. You just let the cries of your heart spill out.

Ephesians was written by someone who really knew how to pray—maybe because he had spent so much time in desperate situations! However he learned, his prayers have the ring of genuineness. Of power. Of true connectedness to God. In our passage today, Ephesians 1:15–19, we're going to study one of Paul's prayers. It's not a long one, but it isn't the length of a prayer that makes it great; the greatest of prayers are those that we voice from the heart. In other words, when we pray like we mean it. And you can't miss the sincerity in the tone of this one. By examining its purpose and meaning, maybe we'll get some ideas for our own prayers.

Paul Praised God for the Ephesians

We won't find Paul's prayer word-for-word in this passage. Instead, we'll read his description of it. Remember, he was writing a letter, and in it he was telling the Ephesians, "I've been praying for you." But he didn't leave it at that. He told them exactly what he'd been saying to God about them. His prayer had two simple parts, and we see them in verse 16:

> [I] do not cease giving thanks for you, while making mention of you in my prayers.

Paul both gave thanks for and made mention of the Ephesians in his prayers. Verse 15 tells us the things he was thankful for:

> I [have] heard of the *faith* in the Lord Jesus which exists among you and your *love* for all the saints. (emphasis added)

Let's take a moment to grasp the significance of their faith and love.

Because of Their Faith

Paul was grateful to God for the Ephesians and for who they had become. He was thankful, first of all, for their faith—not just for the saving faith they had exercised when they first believed but for the continuance of that faith. The Ephesians were sure of their foundation—unlike the man commentator R. Kent Hughes tells us about:

> [The man] was attempting to cross the frozen St. Lawrence River in Canada. Unsure whether the ice would hold, the man first tested it by laying one hand on it. Then he got down on his knees and gingerly began making his way across. When he got to the middle of the frozen river trembling with fear, he heard a noise behind him. Looking back, to his horror he saw a team of horses pulling a carriage down the road toward the river. And upon reaching the river they didn't stop, but bolted right onto the ice and past him, while he crouched there on all fours, turning a deep crimson. If only he had known

how firm the ice really was that day.[2]

Lots of Christians—maybe even most of them—venture into faith as though walking on a thin sheet of ice that covers a rushing river. They tiptoe along, afraid it will crack at any moment and plunge them into the depths. The rushing river is there, all right. But the ice that covers it is thick and unbreakable. The Ephesians knew that nothing could befall them that the Lord wasn't aware of and couldn't cope with. Frigid winds might blow, but the foundation beneath their feet was rock solid, and they lived as though they believed it.

Because of Their Love

Paul was also thankful for what the Ephesians did: they loved the saints. And not just some of the saints, such as the ones who were like them, the ones they felt comfortable with, or the ones they knew. The Ephesians loved *all* of God's people.

Why is it that Christianity sometimes seems to move people away from others? Too many believers get so immersed in their own brand of godly living that they become virtual enemies of those whose godliness looks different from theirs. Churches other than their own may as well not even exist. The Ephesians, though, had their hearts thrown wide open to embrace believers of every variety.

Paul had nurtured these Christians in their faith, and he was profoundly thankful for the fruits of his efforts. But he wasn't blind to the Ephesians' needs, and the next part of his prayer addresses what he desired for them.

Paul's Petitions for the Ephesians

If you've ever lived far away from someone you loved, especially if that someone was in a difficult situation, then you know how Paul felt. Maybe it was when your young, naïve, trusting daughter went away to a secular university. Or when your son was serving overseas with the military. You tend to pray like you mean it in those kinds of situations. It's the only thing you can do. But it's also the *best* thing you can do. And it's what Paul did for the Ephesians, his children in the faith.

2. R. Kent Hughes, *Ephesians: The Mystery of the Body of Christ*, Preaching the Word Series (Wheaton, Ill.: Good News Publishers, Crossway Books, 1990), pp. 49–50.

The Ephesians were rich in faith and love, but Paul longed for them to have another kind of wealth as well. He asked the Lord to let them abound in knowledge and enlightenment.

That They Would Have Full Knowledge of God

The Ephesians obviously knew God, but they were living in a culture where idolatry was rampant, where the lifestyle was licentious, and where those around them took their cues from the Roman emperor, not from the Lord. Paul knew that the Ephesians needed a deeper understanding of God if they were going to hold fast to their identity in Christ, and that is what he asked God to give them:

> [I pray] that the God of our Lord Jesus Christ, the
> Father of glory, may give to you a spirit of wisdom
> and of revelation in the knowledge of Him. (1:17)

What exactly did Paul mean by the phrase "knowledge of Him"? He probably didn't mean that he wanted them to know more *about* God. During his three years with the Ephesians, he had surely given them plenty of information. What they needed was not to know more *about* God, but *to know* God *Himself* more deeply. They needed to feel the sureness of His character and trust in it. They needed to see what was in God's heart:

- His lavish generosity

- His eagerness to bless

- His beautiful holiness

- His infinite kindness and grace

- His desire to accept us as family

This is the kind of knowledge Paul wanted the Ephesians to possess. And he prayed that they would come to this knowledge through "a spirit of wisdom"—discerning insight— "and revelation" —God's unveiling of Himself through His Word and His Spirit.

Some commentators believe that the "spirit of wisdom" to which Paul referred in this verse is the Holy Spirit. While it is true that the Holy Spirit is the source of wisdom and knowledge, it seems more likely that Paul was asking God to give the Ephesians an attitude, or disposition, of wanting to pursue and embrace His wisdom and revelation.[3] This kind of attitude would help them live out the new life to which they had been called (see 4:1).

That They Would Be Enlightened

Paul asked one other thing for the Ephesians: that they would be "enlightened." In other words, he desired that they become more aware of some spiritual realities—three in particular:

> I pray that the eyes of your heart may be enlightened,
> so that you will know what is the hope of His calling,
> what are the riches of the glory of His inheritance
> in the saints, and what is the surpassing greatness of
> His power toward us who believe. (1:18–19a)

First, Paul wanted them to know *the hope of God's calling.* We tend to think of a calling in individual terms, applying it to someone's vocation for a certain type of ministry or lifestyle. But the meaning here is broader than that; it applies to all Christians. Commentator John Stott helps us understand what it means:

> He called us to Christ and holiness, to freedom and peace, to suffering and glory. More simply, it was a call to an altogether new life in which we know, love, obey and serve Christ, enjoy fellowship with him and with each other, and look beyond our present suffering to the glory which will one day be revealed.[4]

When we live in daily harmony with God, we have more than just a vague hope that the future will be positive. Rather, our hope is a complete assurance that God will do all that He has promised and that He can and will bring good from any situation that comes into our lives. Even suffering takes on a new meaning when we realize that the God who has counted every hair on our heads is intimately acquainted with the pain we are experiencing. He is with us in it, and He plans to use it for our benefit and for His glory. When we truly understand that, our attitude changes from resistance to acceptance and we begin to cooperate with the process.

3. For further discussion, please see Harold W. Hoehner, "Ephesians," in *The Bible Knowledge Commentary,* New Testament edition, ed. John F. Walvoord and Roy B. Zuck (Colorado Springs, Colo.: Chariot Victor Publishing, 1983), p. 620.

4. John R. W. Stott, *The Message of Ephesians: God's New Society,* The Bible Speaks Today Series (Downers Grove, Ill.: InterVarsity Press, 1979), p. 56. Used by permission of InterVarsity Press-US and InterVarsity Press-UK.

Paul knew the Ephesians were bound to face some suffering, and he wanted them to be able to face it with true hope.

Paul also wanted them to know *the riches of the glory of His inheritance*. This inheritance consists of all God has given to us in salvation, some of which we possess now, the rest of which we will receive when we meet Him face-to-face. Peter described this inheritance as "imperishable and undefiled [which] will not fade away" (1 Pet. 1:4), and he shared that it is being kept in heaven for us. Can you imagine what that will be like?

In the same verse, Peter affirmed that we will become like Christ. We will no longer sin, and all our human limitations, physical diseases and disabilities, emotional baggage, and every difficulty we have will be gone forever! We will see our Savior in all His glory, and we will be eternally delivered from the adversary. James Montgomery Boice puts it beautifully:

> How little we know of those blessings! We know little enough of the blessings God has for us here, blessings like prayer, Bible study, the joys of Christian fellowship, meaningful work, the sacraments. But if that is true of earthly things, how much truer is it of heavenly things! What do we know of heavenly joys? the new Jerusalem? the beatific vision? Indeed, even Paul wrote, "Now we see but a poor reflection . . . then we shall see face to face. Now I know in part; then I shall know fully, even as I am fully known (1 Cor. 13:12). We know little; and we know imperfectly. But we should know more—and will, as we pray for one another and progress in grace.[5]

Third, Paul wanted the Ephesians to understand *the surpassing greatness of God's power*. The word *power* is *dunamis* in Greek, which means "capability" or "potential." But God's power isn't just potentially great. It is *surpassingly* great. It is *incomparably* great. The word in Greek, *huperballo*, tells us that God's power is so unimaginably great that it belongs in "another sphere altogether."[6]

---

5. James Montgomery Boice, *Ephesians: An Expositional Commentary* (Grand Rapids, Mich.: Baker Books, 1997), p. 37. Used by permission.

6. A. Skevington Wood, "Ephesians," in *The Expositor's Bible Commentary*, gen. ed. Frank E. Gaebelein (Grand Rapids, Mich.: Zondervan Publishing House, Regency Reference Library, 1978), vol. 11, p. 30.

This power is what brings to life that which was dead—it brought Christ out of the tomb (1:20), and it brought us out of sin's sepulchre (2:1–5). Why did Paul want us to know God's power so deeply? So that we would be assured that:

- God is on [our] side, ready to help [us] meet each and every obstacle;

- God's power is never . . . out of commission— it is always actively working on [our] behalf;

- God is always fighting against the forces of evil on believers' behalf;

- no human strength or spiritual power from the evil world (not even Satan himself) can deter or change God's inherent power.[7]

You can't read about Paul's prayer for the Ephesians and miss his passion. He prayed for them like he meant it. And the things he wanted for them are available to us as well . . . when we pray like we mean it!

✣ *Living Insights*

How's your prayer life? Is it holding up pretty well under the load of a busy schedule and a multitude of obligations? Or do most of your prayers seem only to say "Thanks!" or "Help!"?

If that's the case, don't be discouraged, and don't feel guilty. But don't stay there, either, because you'll miss out on an amazing, invigorating experience!

The solution to your prayer problem is not as overwhelming as you might think. You don't have to go to a weeklong seminar or isolate yourself in the woods for a daylong fast. What you *do* need to do is dedicate a little time and energy each day to figuring out what you really want to say to God.

Not sure where to begin? Look again at Paul's prayer:

[I pray] that the God of our Lord Jesus Christ,

7. Bruce B. Barton, Philip Comfort, Kent Keller, Linda K. Taylor, and Dave Veerman, *Ephesians*, Life Application Bible Commentary Series (Wheaton, Ill.: Tyndale House Publishers, 1996), p. 32.

the Father of glory, may give to you a spirit of wisdom
and of revelation in the knowledge of Him. I pray
that the eyes of your heart may be enlightened, so
that you will know what is the hope of His calling,
what are the riches of the glory of His inheritance
in the saints, and what is the surpassing greatness of
His power toward us who believe. (1:17–19a)

What strikes you about this prayer?

_____

_____

_____

_____

_____

_____

What specific things did Paul pray for?

_____

_____

_____

_____

_____

_____

Do you want any of these things for yourself or for some of the
people in your life?

_____

_____

_____

_____

_____

_____

What additional things would you like to pray for?

_____

_____

_____

_____

_____

_____

Now craft your own prayer. The words don't need to be fancy, but they do need to be heartfelt. God is listening!

Chapter 5

WHAT IS CHRIST DOING NOW . . . AND WHY?

Ephesians 1:18–23

Just before World War II, tragedy burned its way through the little town of Itasca, Texas, scorching the hearts of nearly every family who lived there. The local school caught fire, and 263 children died in its heat.

Itasca's residents had neither the drive nor the resources to rebuild the school while the war raged on. But the end of the war brought hope, and soon the walls went up on a new building. The fire was not forgotten, however. This time, the school installed the finest sprinkler system technology could design.

When the project was complete, the townspeople came out in droves to see the facility. Honor students guided visitors through a tour, the highlight of which was the reassuring sight of sprinkler heads standing guard over the heads of the pupils. Parents sent their children to class with confidence, secure in the knowledge that a school fire would never again claim young lives in Itasca.

Just seven years later, though, the town had grown, and already the school needed to be enlarged. As workmen began construction, they discovered an appalling fact.

The best sprinkler system their money could buy had never been connected.[1]

That story makes us shudder. But many Christians live every day with a disconnection of even greater proportions. When we accept Christ's sacrifice on the cross, we gain access to a source of power beyond our comprehension. The might that carved the Grand Canyon, the might that heaved the stone away from the tomb, is at our disposal. It stands ready to enable us to overcome temptation. It's available when depression overtakes us or when life's troubles overwhelm us. But if we don't connect to it, we're just about as good as those waterless sprinklers.

---

1. See R. Kent Hughes, *Ephesians: The Mystery of the Body of Christ*, Preaching the Word Series (Wheaton, Ill.: Good News Publishers, Crossway Books, 1990), p. 57.

In the previous chapter, we read Paul's initial description of God's power. In this passage, we'll study his expanded explanation. And we'll go a step further, looking at why we tend to get disconnected from that power and how we can go about turning it back on in our lives.

God's Power Personified

In Ephesians 1, Paul let us eavesdrop on his prayer for the Ephesians. We read of his heartfelt request that

> the eyes of [their] heart may be enlightened, so that [they] will know what is the hope of His calling, what are the riches of the glory of His inheritance in the saints, and what is the surpassing greatness of His power toward us who believe. (vv. 18–19a)

He then elaborated that the source of all these things was found in "the working of the strength of His might" (v. 19b).

In verse 20, Paul assured us of God's enormous power by reminding us of Christ's Resurrection and Ascension:

> He raised Him from the dead and seated Him at His right hand in the heavenly places, far above all rule and authority and power and dominion, and every name that is named, not only in this age but also in the one to come. And He put all things in subjection under His feet, and gave Him as head over all things to the church, which is His body, the fullness of Him who fills all in all. (vv. 20b–23)

If we look closely at this beautiful passage, we'll see that Paul offered us four proofs to pin our confidence on.

"He Raised Him from the Dead"

The Resurrection story is so familiar to us that we tend to take it for granted. We cease to really see the corpse that was Christ, first hanging on the cross, and then wrapped, mummylike, in the cave. We forget what He would have looked like, having been beaten, tortured, and finally stabbed with a sword. And so we miss the significance of a walking, breathing, scarred—but completely healed—Jesus talking with loved ones just a few days later.

Medical technology has progressed incredibly since the time of

42

Christ, but even today this kind of transformation, even of someone merely injured, let alone dead, is unfathomable. Yet God accomplished it! The Resurrection is unquestionably God's power on display.

"He . . . Seated Him at His Right Hand"

After raising Christ from the dead, God exalted Him to the place of highest honor—at His own right hand. Although Paul used a physical image here, he probably intended his readers to view the "right hand" more as symbol of authority than as an actual place.[2] The Life Application Bible Commentary puts it this way:

> According to ancient practice, the seat at the right hand signified a position of equality. Christ will remain there until all his enemies have been overcome (1 Corinthians 15:25). His remaining seated symbolizes his finished work and supreme authority.[3]

Remember, Christ left His heavenly throne in order to accomplish our salvation. After His death, when He left His physical body behind, the Father restored Him to that position of authority equal to His own.

"He Put All Things in Subjection under His Feet"

Jesus' appointment to sit at the Father's right hand is known as "the doctrine of Session,"[4] and it was prophesied by King David in Psalm 110:

> The Lord says to my Lord:
> "Sit at My right hand
> Until I make Your enemies a footstool for Your feet."
> (v. 1)

Being at the Father's right hand meant more than the restoration

---

2. See A. Skevington Wood, "Ephesians," in *The Expositor's Bible Commentary*, gen. ed. Frank E. Gaebelein (Grand Rapids, Mich.: Zondervan Publishing House, Regency Reference Library, 1978), vol. 11, p. 30.

3. Bruce B. Barton, Philip Comfort, Kent Keller, Linda K. Taylor, and Dave Veerman, *Ephesians*, Life Application Bible Commentary Series (Wheaton, Ill.: Tyndale House Publishers, 1996), p. 32.

4. See *Evangelical Dictionary of Theology*, ed. Walter A. Elwell (Grand Rapids, Mich.: Baker Book House, 1984), p. 1007.

of Christ's position. It also meant having power. David went on to say that Jesus would

> shatter kings in the day of His wrath.
> He will judge among the nations,
> He will fill them with corpses,
> He will shatter the chief men over a broad country.
> (vv. 5–6)

The act of exalting Christ displays God's power. And the coming judgment will reveal Christ's own power. But Christ's power is not merely relegated to the future. In Ephesians 1:21, Paul told us that the exalted Christ rules even now over all things, including His enemies and everything seen and unseen, in heaven and on earth. Every single thing that comes into our lives is under Christ's power—the good and the bad, the past and the present, and even the future. Isn't that a comforting thought?

"He . . . Gave Him as Head over All Things to the Church"

God has given Christ power not only over our individual lives but over our lives together as His body, the church (v. 22).

Think about the almost unbelievable benefits this brings to us as believers: The King who sits on the throne of the universe is also our Brother and our Mediator before the Father (see Rom. 8:29; 1 Tim. 2:5; Heb. 9:15). What do we have to fear with Him on our side, defending us and watching over us? Nothing!

God's Power Put to Work

We've seen God's power at work in Christ. Now let's see why we need to tap into that power.

In verse 21, Paul told us that Christ sits above "all rule and authority and power and dominion." Do these words sound familiar? If you're familiar with Ephesians, you may recognize them from the sixth chapter, where Paul clarified that

> our struggle is not against flesh and blood, but against
> the rulers, against the powers, against the world forces
> of this darkness, against the spiritual forces of wick-
> edness in the heavenly places. (v. 12)

In both passages, Paul was talking about the supernatural realm —the places and personalities beyond our known world. Christ doesn't merely rule over the earth and its people; He also rules over the spiritual world and its inhabitants.

Some of these personalities have made themselves His enemies and currently war against Him and His followers. In other words, they war against *us!* Unseen, demonic foes are trying to destroy us, but thankfully God let us in on their weapons and tactics. We'll study Ephesians 6 in more depth later on, but let's take a quick look at it right now to get an idea of what we're up against.

First, *our enemies battle against us.* Paul used the term *struggle—palē* in Greek—in verse 12 to describe the way these evil forces engage us. The word literally means "wrestle." The battle we fight with these attackers is not abstract; it's an in-your-face, grabbing, pushing, eye-gouging match of strength and will. They're on us whether we like it or not.

Second, *our enemies have a method.* In verse 11, Paul said that the Devil "schemes" against us. This word, *methodia* in Greek, is the term from which we get our word *method.* John Stott suggests that Satan has a strategy.[5] Does it surprise you to realize that his attacks are not haphazard but plotted and planned? With militaristic order and discipline, his minions work every day to expose our weaknesses, undermine our confidence, and infiltrate our congregations.

Third, *our enemies are formidable.* Commentator John MacArthur describes the extent of their destructive force:

> Satan's forces of darkness are highly organized and structured for the most destructive warfare possible. . . . They are a great and ancient multitude and constitute a formidable and highly experienced supernatural enemy.
>
> The demonic categories [given by Paul in v. 12] are not explained, but *rulers* no doubt reflects a high order of demons (linked with "authorities" in Col. 2:15), *powers* are another rank (mentioned in 1 Pet. 3:22), and *world forces of this darkness* perhaps refers to demons who have infiltrated various political systems of the world.[6]

5. John R. W. Stott, *The Message of Ephesians: God's New Society,* The Bible Speaks Today Series (Downers Grove, Ill.: InterVarsity Press, 1979), p. 265.

6. John MacArthur, *Ephesians,* The MacArthur New Testament Commentary Series (Chicago, Ill.: Moody Press, 1986), p. 341.

Starting to feel the need for God's strength? Well, rest assured—we've got it! With Christ at our side, we have all the power we need to withstand Satan's attacks and win the fight.

God's Power on Display

Despite our need to live in God's unmatched power, we so often don't. Why? Simple—we get disconnected from Him. Sometimes we make the mistake of thinking we can handle things on our own. After all, we're smart people. We have loads of resolve. We know how to solve problems, overcome obstacles, and endure hardships. So we try to handle our problems on our own strength.

But we reawaken to the hard slap of reality when Satan finds the chink in our armor and pierces us through with a problem deeper than our own resources. We're no match for him, and the only way to resist him is to tap into God's power and rely on His strength.

The Greatest Evidence of Power Is Change

How can we tell when we're connected to God's power? Our lives will grow and develop. Have you seen ways in which you've matured spiritually? Have the fruits of the Spirit become more visible in you (Gal. 5:22–23)? God has produced that growth. Like the life force within a seed that causes the seedling to sprout and eventually burst forth with fruit, God's power works inside our hearts to produce love, joy, and peace.

God's Power Is Best Displayed in Weakness

Interestingly, the most fertile soil for our growth is not good times but difficult times, times of weakness and doubt. Our weakest moments are our strongest allies in learning to depend on God. It sounds contradictory, but it couldn't be more true. Paul himself experienced a "thorn in the flesh," a condition that plagued him without relief (2 Cor. 12:7). Yet it was this very condition that forced him to grow in his ability to lean on God's power (v. 9a). As a result, the apostle boasted about his weaknesses, knowing that in them, God's power showed up best (v. 9b). And because of them, Paul continually sought God's power rather than relying on himself.

Paul's attitude reveals an important principle: *The greater our acknowledged weakness, the more evident Christ's enabling strength.* To connect with God's power, we must first admit our own inadequacy and turn each and every situation over to Him. Only then is His power free to flow in, through, and around us . . . and He gets all the glory.

🙶 Living Insights

The great Charles Haddon Spurgeon once implored his listeners,

> Dear brothers and sisters, go home and never ask the Lord to make you strong in yourselves, never ask Him to make you anybody or anything, but be content to be nothing and nobody. Next ask that His power may have room in you, and that all those who come near you may see what God can do by nothings and nobodies. . . . Live with this desire, to glorify God.[7]

Do you sometimes feel inadequate? If you do, take heart—you're well on your way to tapping into God's strength and living a life of victory and joy! You see, God can't empower people who live under their own power. And He can't glorify Himself through people who seek glory for themselves. Only through the weak can He show His strength, and only through the humble can He reveal His glory.

The meek and humble in heart experience the Christian life as God designed it. If this weren't true, the Messiah would have been born the son of a king, not a carpenter; He would have born in a palace, not a stable.

Most of us, however, probably stand somewhere in the middle. We haven't yet come to that hour of desperation when we can do nothing else but fall on our faces before God. But neither do we feel as though we've lived our lives totally on our own. We've tried to rely on Him, yet we long to get closer, to strengthen that connection. In order to do that, take a few minutes to evaluate your own life, to see how closely you've kept that connection.

On a scale of one to ten, whose strength have you been relying on? (1 = all on self; 10 = all on God)

1 2 3 4 5 6 7 8 9 10

7. Charles Haddon Spurgeon, *The Treasury of the Bible* (Grand Rapids, Mich.: Zondervan Publishing House, 1968), vol. 7, pp. 276–77.

Based on what you've learned in this chapter, what can you do to move your score to the right? Consider how you can . . .

- Trust more completely in the extent of God's power:

  _____

  _____

  _____

  _____

  _____

  _____

  _____

- Remind yourself of your need to rely on His strength and not your own:

  _____

  _____

  _____

  _____

  _____

  _____

  _____

Chapter 6

YOU WERE DEAD . . . BUT GOD!

Ephesians 2:1–9

S ome years ago, pastor R. Kent Hughes and his group of high schoolers hiked to the top of Mount Whitney in California, the highest spot in the continental United States (14,494 feet). They were exhilarated by the breathtaking panorama of the Sierra Nevada mountains and the Mojave Desert below.

"What a spot," Hughes exulted, "with its rarefied, crystal-clear air, its indigo and turquoise lakes—vista giving way to vista as far as one could see." [1]

As the group surveyed the world from that pinnacle, one of the teens mentioned that Death Valley, the lowest point in the United States, lay only eighty miles away. In less than a hundred miles, you could travel from a height of over 14,000 feet to a drop of 282 feet below sea level—from crisp mountain air to a suffocating 134 degrees in the shade. Hughes remarked,

> What a contrast! One place is the top of the world, the other the bottom. One place is perpetually cool, the other relentlessly hot. From Mt. Whitney you look down on all of life. From Death Valley you can only look up to the rest of the world. [2]

It's hard to imagine a starker contrast, but one does exist—not in the physical world but in the spiritual. In Ephesians 2, Paul described the "Death Valley" all of us are born into (vv. 1–3), as well as the glorious change of location God has provided through Jesus' death and Resurrection (vv. 4–9). Christ has rescued us from the desert and exalted us to a spiritual "Mount Whitney"!

As you prepare to survey our spiritual landscape, take care— the stark, barren state of our souls before Christ may be overwhelm-

---

1. R. Kent Hughes, *Ephesians: The Mystery of the Body of Christ*, Preaching the Word Series (Wheaton, Ill.: Good News Publishers, Crossway Books, 1990), p. 65.

2. Hughes, *Ephesians*, p. 65.

ingly bleak. But the "rarefied, crystal-clear air" of God's grace will soon set your heart soaring in awestruck gratitude!

The Howling Desert Wasteland

Whether we knew it or not, we wandered through the desolate wasteland of spiritual death before Christ came into our lives:

> And you were dead in your trespasses and sins, in which you formerly walked according to the course of this world, according to the prince of the power of the air, of the spirit that is now working in the sons of disobedience. Among them we too all formerly lived in the lusts of our flesh, indulging the desires of the flesh and of the mind, and were by nature children of wrath, even as the rest. (vv. 1–3)

Let's take a closer look at Paul's description of our desolate condition.

We Were Dead

You were dead in your trespasses and sins. (v. 1)

Though outwardly we looked very much alive, inside we were cut off from life because we were cut off from God, the Author of life. Sin was the quicksand foundation of our lives, and no matter how good we tried to be, we couldn't extricate ourselves from its relentless, sucking, downward pull.

We Walked in Satan's Way

> You formerly walked according to the course of this world, according to the prince of the power of the air, of the spirit that is now working in the sons of disobedience. Among them we too all formerly lived in the lusts of our flesh, indulging the desires of the flesh and of the mind. (vv. 2–3a)

Most people like to think they go their own way, chart their own course—sort of the "I am the master of my fate: I am the captain of my soul"[3] school of thought. How shocking, then, to

---

3. William Ernest Henley, "Invictus," as quoted in *The Best Loved Poems of the American People*, comp. Hazel Felleman (Garden City, N.Y.: Doubleday and Co., Garden City Publishers, 1936), p. 73.

find that if we walked apart from God, we actually walked in Satan's insidious company, or, as Paul called him, "the prince of the power of the air."

Yes, there is a literal Satan and a literal demonic host, manipulating minds and controlling wills, telling us, "Truth is a lie . . . lies are the truth." When we thought we were blazing our own trail, in truth we were following Satan.

Where do the Devil and his world system lead us? Into disobedience of God—into a life dominated by our own selfishness and willfulness, our glands and our greed.[4] In contrast to God's kingdom law of love, where we care about others' needs and actively work for their best interests, Satan's style is to encourage us to get what we want, no matter the cost. And the ultimate cost is terrifying.

We Stood Condemned

[We] were by nature children of wrath, even as the rest. (v. 3b)

As unredeemed sinners, we stood condemned to eternal separation from God. Like guilty prisoners with too many charges to count, we waited before the Judge of the universe without hope. His wrath against sin—a "holy, just revulsion against what is contrary to and opposes his holy nature and will"[5]—demands that sin be justly punished. Jesus described the end result of God's wrath as Gehenna or hell: a place of "outer darkness" and "weeping and gnashing of teeth" "where their worm does not die, and the fire is not quenched" (Matt. 8:12; Mark 9:44, 46, 48). J. I. Packer explains the horror of these images:

> The "worm" that "dieth not" . . . [was] an image, it seems, for the endless dissolution of the personality by a condemning conscience; "fire" for the agonising awareness of God's displeasure; "outer darkness" for knowledge of the loss, not merely of God, but of all

4. Commentator Charles Hodge adds an important point: "We do not know how . . . [Satan's evil] spirits have access to our minds to control their operations. The influence, whatever it is, . . . does not destroy our freedom of action, any more than the influence of one man over his fellows." *Commentary on the Epistle to the Ephesians* (1857; reprint, Grand Rapids, Mich.: William B. Eerdmans Publishing Co., 1994), p. 103.

5. Walter W. Wessel, note on Romans 1:18 in *The NIV Study Bible*, gen. ed. Kenneth L. Barker (Grand Rapids, Mich.: Zondervan Bible Publishers, 1985), p. 1707.

good, and everything that made life seem worth living; "gnashing of teeth" for self-condemnation and self-loathing.[6]

Praise God for providing a way out of this nightmare!

The Mountain of the Lord

What did God do to rescue us from sin, death, and condemnation? Paul eagerly gave us the good news in Ephesians 2:4–6:

> But God, being rich in mercy, because of His great love with which He loved us, even when we were dead in our transgressions, made us alive together with Christ (by grace you have been saved), and raised us up with Him, and seated us with Him in the heavenly places in Christ Jesus.

Talk about a change in altitude! God plucked us from the desert and set us on a mountaintop. Not even a peak like Mount Whitney reaches as high as our new position—a seat in heaven itself! Look at what He's done for us:

- *"But God . . . made us alive."* The only way spiritually dead people can have a relationship with God is to have a spiritual resurrection. And God is the only One who can accomplish that, which He did through His Son. Christ defeated sin and death through His own death and Resurrection and, as a result, can give us spiritual life. J. I. Packer vividly explains, "Between us sinners and the thunder-clouds of divine wrath stands the cross of the Lord Jesus." He is "our substitute and sin-bearer,"[7] transferring us from death to life (see John 5:24; Col. 2:13–14).

- *"But God . . . raised us up."* As God raised Jesus from the depths of the tomb to new, incorruptible life, so He has lifted us from the dank depths of sin to new life in Christ. We not only look forward to our future physical resurrection and glorification, but we also participate in our new righteous and hopeful

---

6. J. I. Packer, *Knowing God* (Downers Grove, Ill.: InterVarsity Press, 1973), p. 138. Packer's chapter "The Wrath of God" provides an outstanding explanation of this sometimes difficult topic.

7. Packer, *Knowing God*, p. 141.

life here and now, which became available to us the moment we believed (see Col. 2:12).

- *"But God . . . seated us with Him in the heavenly places."* We know that Christ sits at the Father's right hand (Eph. 1:20), but isn't it amazing to know that we, too, have a place in heaven— *right now* (see Phil. 3:20)? We have a permanent citizenship in heaven that gives us hope and helps us live for God during our time here on earth.

Notice the contrast with our former way of life: We were dead, *but God* made us alive; we were mired in sin, *but God* raised us to a new, clean life; we were destined for hell, *but God* seated us next to His own Son in heaven. We were helpless to do any of this, *but God* did it all through Christ!

Why Did God Do It?

Why would God go to such great lengths to rescue dead, sin-entrenched people? Not because underneath it all we're so wonderful—but because above all *He's* so wonderful!

He is "rich in mercy" (Eph. 2:4a). The Lord abounds in tender compassion and overflows with merciful kindness. His heart's desire is to give us what we need rather than what we deserve.

The Lord also has "great love" for us. And what greater picture of love do we have than God's taking on our flesh, living with us, teaching us, and finally stretching out His arms on a cross to take on death in our place? The thorns, the lashed and bleeding back, the nails, the stab wound in His side . . . the tears—each of these portrays the love that bore all things, believed all things, hoped all things, and endured all things to secure our salvation (see 1 Cor. 13:7).

And God is also gracious and kind:

> So that in the ages to come He might show the
> surpassing riches of His grace in kindness toward us
> in Christ Jesus. (Eph. 2:7)

If all the treasures of the sea, if all the gold, silver, diamonds, rubies, and emeralds of the earth could be heaped into one towering pile, they would amount to a speck of dust next to the immense riches of God's grace and kindness! We who are redeemed by Jesus are a shining testimony to the marvelous grace of God to all generations.

How Did God Do It?

Grace not only moved God's heart, but it also moved us from death to life:

> For by grace you have been saved through faith; and
> that not of yourselves, it is the gift of God; not as
> a result of works, so that no one may boast. (vv. 8–9)

Grace was both the *motive* and the *means* through which God saved us. Our salvation was accomplished not by our works—we were helpless to do anything—but by His gift of grace. He initiated it, He implemented it, and He receives all the glory for it. You might find it helpful to remember what grace is all about in this acrostic: God's Riches at Christ's Expense.

Grace is also God reaching out to offer cool, living water for our desert-parched lips.

Thoughts for the Road

What an incredible message the Lord has given us through Paul's pen! All because of God's grace, we have moved from death to life, from corruption to redemption, from hell to heaven.

But remember, even though Christ has brought us out of the blistering desert to His cool mountaintop, we still live among many who suffer in the desert wastes. They may look happy and fulfilled outwardly, but inwardly they desperately need the life-giving touch of God's grace. They may not even be aware of that, but because of what Paul has taught us, we are aware of it now. So let's be channels of God's grace to others by embracing it ourselves and resting in the joyous relief only His gift of grace can bring.

Living Insights

God never intended His grace to remain an abstract theological concept; rather, He meant it to become a very real force in our lives. So, with this in mind, let's get personal about God's grace.

What are some times when God has shown you grace? For example, when did He provide for you in a special way or sustain you through a hard time? Describe it.

_____

_____

_____

How did His kindness toward you change your relationship with Him? Did it motivate you to trust Him more, to step out in faith, to commit more of your life to Him? Be specific.

_____

_____

_____

_____

Describe a time in your past when another person showed you an undeserved kindness.

_____

_____

_____

_____

How did it affect your feelings toward that person? Toward life?

_____

_____

_____

_____

As God's ambassadors, we're called to reflect His grace to the world—especially in the way we treat people. We can draw them to the Lord by showering them with grace, just as He did with us. We can become the face of God's grace!

Think about this truth as you go through your day, and see the difference grace makes in your life and in the lives of others. It may bring someone out of the desert and up to the mountain of God's salvation.

Chapter 7

GOD'S ARTWORK ON DISPLAY
Ephesians 2:10

On August 22, 1741, a man named Charles Jennens delivered a collection of Bible verses to a composer-friend of his, George Handel. "Can you make an entertainment out of it?" he asked. Author Hertha Pauli records the answer:

> As soon as Jennens had left, the Master started reading the text he had received. The words, Handel noticed, were all taken from the Scriptures; but in arranging the quotations, the Master felt, Jennens had outdone himself. The words seemed to sing by themselves.
>
> Handel started writing at once. He wrote so fast that the ink had scarcely dried on one page before he started another. The score was covered with splotches, but the Master did not notice them. He forgot the whole world around him.
>
> "Whether I was in my body or out of my body as I wrote *The Messiah*," Handel said later, "I know not."
>
> For twenty-four days he remained in the little front room on the first floor of his house near Hanover Square in London, setting down thousands of notes to Jennens' biblical excerpts. At regular intervals Handel's servant brought him food, but the Master left it untouched. Sometimes the servant stood in silent wonder as the Master's tears fell on a page and mingled with the ink while he penned his notes. And once the servant found the Master sobbing with emotion. He had just finished the "Hallelujah Chorus."
>
> "I thought I saw all Heaven before me," Handel told his choir boys, "and the great God himself!"[1]

---

1. Hertha Pauli, *Handel and the Messiah Story* (New York, N.Y.: Meredith Press, 1968), pp. 49, 51.

Handel's *Messiah* has enraptured audiences for over 250 years and is considered Handel's finest work. But what if his masterpiece had never been published? What if the composer had rolled up his composition and locked it in a cabinet, shutting away the melodies and lyrics in his own mind and sharing them with no one?

If he had, one of music history's greatest achievements would have been lost. The world never would have experienced the serenity of his Airs, the grandeur of his "Pastoral Symphony," or the spine-tingling inspiration of his "Hallelujah Chorus." What a tragedy!

Similar to Handel's *Messiah*, each one of us is an inspired creation. God has inscribed His symphony of grace on our hearts like notes on a musical score. And like an artistic genius whose joy is complete when his work is shared, our Composer intends His work of art to be heard . . . and seen.

The Purpose of God's Artwork

> For we are His workmanship, created in Christ Jesus
> for good works, which God prepared beforehand so
> that we would walk in them. (Eph. 2:10)

We are God's "workmanship," His masterpiece. What a wonderful thing to know about ourselves! But unlike statues or paintings that simply adorn the halls of museums, we're designed for action. God has good works for us to do that He "prepared beforehand"— before we were saved, even before we were born.

From His sovereign seat, God foresaw us resting in His protection and boldly taking a stand against evil, compassionately extending a hand to the needy, and lovingly sharing the gospel every time He gives us a chance. His plan for our lives extends beyond salvation to sanctification, beyond standing in grace to walking in good deeds.

The works God has in mind for us may sometimes seem bigger than we can handle; His Word issues some mighty tall orders. How can we live up to them?

If we think that we lack the courage or power to put our faith into action, Bible teacher Warren Wiersbe encourages us with this reminder:

> The same resurrection power that saved you and
> took you out of the graveyard of sin can daily help
> you live for Christ and glorify Him. At great expense
> to Himself, God worked for us on the cross. And

today, on the basis of that price paid at Calvary, He is working in us to conform us to Christ.[2]

Through Christ, we have the power to become beautiful displays of God's glory. But remember, that power won't help us if we're trying to operate in our own strength. To release God's power, we need to abide in His love by absorbing His words in Scripture and feeding ourselves through prayer. It's impossible to squeeze out good works from hearts that are spiritually parched. Good works are fruits that grow best when we're filled up and nourished with Christ.

The Free Gift of Becoming God's Artwork

With all this talk of good works, it's tempting to think our works somehow contribute to our salvation. Let's resist that temptation.

Paul stated that we were "created" by God. This verb describes actions performed only by the Lord. He first created us while we were in the womb, and then He re-created us at the moment of our belief. That's why Paul stated in 2 Corinthians that anyone who is in Christ is a *new* creation (5:17).

Paul confirmed this truth from another angle in Ephesians 2:8–9, stressing that we could do nothing to contribute to or deserve our re-creation (salvation). It's a wonderful *gift* from God.

Not everyone, though, feels comfortable taking something for free; many of us have had to work hard for everything we've got. But salvation is beyond our power to earn. Eugene Peterson gets to the heart of this in his paraphrase of Paul's words to the Romans:

> If you're a hard worker and do a good job, you deserve your pay; we don't call your wages a gift. But if you see that the job is too big for you, that it's something only *God* can do, and you trust him to do it—you could never do it for yourself no matter how hard and long you worked—well, that trusting-him-to-do-it is what gets you set right with God, by God. Sheer gift.[3] (Rom. 4:4–5 THE MESSAGE)

2. Warren W. Wiersbe, *Be Rich: Are You Losing the Things That Money Can't Buy?* (Wheaton, Ill.: Scripture Press Publications, Victor Books, 1977), p. 47.

3. Eugene H. Peterson, *The Message: The New Testament in Contemporary English* (Colorado Springs, Colo.: NavPress, 1993), p. 310.

Sheer gift—isn't that great? Our salvation is totally free, completely accomplished by God, and open-handedly given to us. We don't have to work for it—we *can't* work for it—we can only rest and rejoice in it!

God's Work Is Performance Art

Then what is the role of good works in our lives? Our works have several crucial purposes. They

- glorify God, especially when Christ is the source of and motive for our actions (see John 15:5, 8; 2 Cor. 9:13; 1 Pet. 2:12).

- showcase the truth of Christ's claims, proving the gospel's authenticity and power (see Phil. 2:14–16; 1 Thess. 2:1–12).

- bring God's loving touch to people (see John 13:34–35; 1 Cor. 13; 1 John 3:17–19).

- promote peace and order in our churches and society (see Jer. 29:7; 1 Tim. 2:1–4; 1 Pet. 2:13–17).

Do you see the connection between grace and works more clearly now—how the two differ and how they complement each other? Works don't contribute to our salvation, but they fulfill the reason for which we were created. They glorify God, help us reveal Him to the world, and testify to the reality of our faith.

What does a life of good works look like? Commentator James Montgomery Boice sheds light on some of the marks of a changed person:

> Because our hearts have been remade we now give food to the hungry, water to the thirsty, homes to the strangers, clothes to the naked, care to the sick, and comfort to those who are in prison—as Jesus said we must do, if we are to sit with him in glory.[4] (see Matt. 25:31–46)

Made alive by Christ, His life now flows through us and streams out in our good works. This truth can safeguard us against becoming prideful in our service. Think of it this way: God wants us to keep

---

4. James Montgomery Boice, *Ephesians: An Expositional Commentary* (Grand Rapids, Mich.: Baker Books, 1997), p. 74. Used by permission.

our eyes, ears, and hearts open to see, hear, and empathize with others' needs *so that He* can respond to those needs through us.

Credit Goes to the Creator

Since this is God's work, He should get the credit, right? Unfortunately, we don't always give it to Him. This world's tendency—and often ours as well—is to exalt human effort. And while recognition and praise when we deserve it affirms and encourages us, we must take caution against exaltation. Our human nature craves the feeding of its appetite for glory—its voracious hunger for receiving all the credit. When we find ourselves desiring and seeking these things, we need this reminder: It's all from Him. Without God in us, no truly good works would be possible.

We are God's workmanship, His masterpieces. As the beauty of artwork testifies to the skill of the artist, so does God's work in us laud Him with praise and glory. To God be the glory, great things He has done—and will do—in us!

❧ *Living Insights*

If you wanted to become a great artist, you'd most likely visit a museum to study the work of the masters, right? After all, emulation is not only the highest form of flattery, it's also the greatest means of mastery.

Likewise, if we want to shape our lives into works of art for God, we need to study the life of our Master, Jesus Christ. The Gospel of John highlights seven specific good works He performed while on earth. As you watch Him work, write down what you see. What aspects of the Father and His plan does He reveal? What do you learn about Jesus' heart?

John 2:1–11 _____

_____

_____

John 4:46–54 _____

_____

_____

John 5:1–17 _____

_____

_____

John 6:1–14 _____

_____

_____

John 6:15–21 _____

_____

_____

John 9:1–12 _____

_____

_____

John 11:1–44 _____

_____

_____

We probably won't perform many miracles, but our hearts and hands can still reach for the same goal as Christ's:

> Therefore many other signs Jesus also performed in the presence of the disciples, which are not written in this book; but these have been written *so that you may believe that Jesus is the Christ, the Son of God; and that believing you may have life in His name.* (20:30–31, emphasis added)

What good works do you regularly engage in?

_____

_____

_____

_____

Do you think others see more of you or more of Christ in those works? Why?

_____

_____

_____

_____

_____

Did you see something in Christ's heart that you need in yours so others can see Him more clearly and seek new life in Him?

_____

_____

_____

_____

_____

Spend some time in prayer, asking the Lord to clarify your direction, purify your motives, and enlarge your heart. And thank Him for His artistry in your life!

Chapter 8

BREAKING DOWN
THE BARRIER

Ephesians 2:11–16

On a hot summer day in 1987, President Ronald Reagan stepped up to a Berlin podium and publicly challenged his Soviet counterpart, General Secretary Mikhail Gorbachev:

> If you seek peace, if you seek prosperity for the So-
> viet Union and Eastern Europe, if you seek liberal-
> ization: come here, to this gate.
> Mr. Gorbachev, open this gate.
> Mr. Gorbachev, tear down this wall.[1]

It's hard to imagine a more difficult task than what the president called for. For twenty-six years, since 1961, the Berlin Wall had stood as a visible icon of separation—a division that was not only physical but also philosophical. A mass of concrete, barbed wire, and stone, it separated the world into two minds—that of the Soviet Union and that of the free world.

Yet, just two years after Reagan's address, Gorbachev met his challenge. When sentries laid down their rifles on Gorbachev's orders, citizens from both sides took up their picks and jackhammers and began tearing down the wall.

Even this great feat, however, can't match what Jesus accomplished when He, through His work on the cross, tore down the wall that separated the Jews and Gentiles (Eph. 2:14). This wall had stood for centuries, representing not political separation but spiritual alienation. God had poured out His cup of blessing into the hands of Abraham and his descendants, the *Jews*. The laws of Moses and the sacrificial system had formed God's pathway for holy living for *Jews*. Gentiles stood outside the gate of salvation, destined to live in spiritual poverty and to die in a state of eternal separation from God. But all that changed when Christ tore down the wall.

Let's look at what Paul had to say about this momentous event,

---

1. National Archives and Records Administration, "Kennedy at the Berlin Wall," accessed September 11, 2000: available at http://www.nara.gov/exhall/originals/kennedy.html.

and let's particularly examine where the Gentiles stood, what the Savior did for them, and why we can be so grateful for what He did.

Where the Gentiles Stood

Paul's letter explains the Gentiles' predicament:

> Therefore remember that formerly you, the Gentiles in the flesh, who are called "Uncircumcision" by the so-called "Circumcision," which is performed in the flesh by human hands—remember that you were at that time separate from Christ, excluded from the commonwealth of Israel, and strangers to the covenants of promise, having no hope and without God in the world. (vv. 11–12)

Separate . . . excluded . . . strangers . . . no hope . . . without God. Before Christ crumbled the dividing wall, this was what life was like for the Gentiles. Their spiritual estrangement was bleaker than a Siberian exile.

Without Christ

Paul first characterized the Gentiles as *separate from Christ.* The Jews always had the hope of a Messiah, the Christ. Their Scriptures revealed that He had been in God's plans since the beginning (Gen. 3:15) and that He would come from their people (2 Sam. 7:13, 16; Isa. 9:1–7; Jer. 33:14–17). The Lord also assured them through His prophets that the Messiah would save them from their sins, conquer their enemies, and lead them into the presence of the Father (Isa. 53:4–12; 54:11–17). The Gentiles, however, had no such promise of a future Messiah.

Without a Home

Paul added that the Gentiles were *excluded from the commonwealth of Israel,* or without a spiritual home. A wall of exclusion stronger than the Berlin wall kept them apart from Israel's privileged relationship with God. This wall took literal form in Herod's temple.

Under Herod's design, the Jewish priests had the closest access to the Lord, with their courtyard built nearest the temple building. The men of Israel were in the courtyard beyond them, and Jewish women worshiped beyond the men. Two walls and a number of steps down later, you'd reach the Court of the Gentiles. The Gentiles could look up at the temple, but that was as close as they were allowed. Notices posted on the thick stone barrier between them and the Jews read "Trespassers Will Be Executed."[2]

To say that the Gentiles were cut off is an enormous understatement!

Without the Covenants

The Gentiles also hadn't received any of the promises God had made to the Jews. These promises included the Abrahamic covenant (Gen. 12:1–3; 15:18–21; 17:1–8), the Palestinian covenant (Deut. 28–30), the Davidic covenant (2 Sam. 7:8–16; Ps. 89), and the new covenant (Jer. 31:31–34; Ezek. 36:22–30). These promises, all pointing to the Messiah and the blessings that would come through Him, assured Israel of their national existence, land, king, and spiritual inheritance.[3] The covenants reminded them of their past and promised them a future. But because the Gentiles did not receive these promises, they could not claim either.

Without Hope

No Savior. No home. No promises. Without these things, the Gentiles had *no hope*. Since the promise of a future rested with the Messiah, they couldn't expect things to get any better—in this life or the next. They were faced with the same conclusion that Satan was in Milton's *Paradise Lost*: "Our final hope is flat despair."[4]

Without God

If the Gentiles had no Savior, no home, no future, and no hope, it could mean only one thing: they had no God. Though they had many gods, those "deities" were powerless to save them from their hopeless, God-less situation.

The Difference Christ Made

The Gentiles' lives and destinies were unbelievably bleak before

---

2. See John R. W. Stott, *The Message of Ephesians: God's New Society,* The Bible Speaks Today Series (Downers Grove, Ill.: InterVarsity Press, 1979), pp. 91–92.

3. See Harold W. Hoehner, "Ephesians," in *The Bible Knowledge Commentary*, New Testament edition, ed. John F. Walvoord and Roy B. Zuck (Colorado Springs, Colo.: Chariot Victor Publishing, 1983), p. 625.

4. John Milton, as quoted by James Montgomery Boice in *Ephesians: An Expositional Commentary* (Grand Rapids, Mich.: Baker Books, 1997), p. 80. Used by permission.

Christ. Thankfully, the Lord tore down the obstacles that blocked the Gentiles from reaching Christ, and He removed forever their sentence of darkness and eternal death. We can give thanks as well because without Christ, our situation was the same as theirs.

He Brought the Far-Off Near

> But now in Christ Jesus you who formerly were far off have been brought near by the blood of Christ. (Eph. 2:13)

Christ first brought the far-off near to Him. He made it possible for the Gentiles—and all unbelievers today—to approach Him through faith. How? *By His blood.* Redemption could come only through Christ's death (see Heb. 9:22); sin's penalty had to be justly paid. Once the estrangement of sin was removed by forgiveness—by His blood Christ made possible remission of sins and reconciliation with God—any who trust in Christ's sacrifice are invited into God's family to enjoy intimacy with Him and with others of His household.

He Brought Peace to the Divided

> For He Himself is our peace, who made both groups into one and broke down the barrier of the dividing wall, by abolishing in His flesh the enmity, which is the Law of commandments contained in ordinances, so that in Himself He might make the two into one new man, thus establishing peace, and might reconcile them both in one body to God through the cross, by it having put to death the enmity. (Eph. 2:14–16)

Christ not only created peace between God and His creation, He also created a new humanity made up of reconciled Jews and Gentiles: He "made both groups into one and broke down the barrier of the dividing wall . . . that in Himself He might make the two into one new man" (vv. 14, 15b). By His death, Jesus gave Jews and Gentiles alike access to God and unity with each other in the church.

So, all Christians stand on level ground before the Cross: young and old, male and female, Jew and Gentile, rich and poor. We all need salvation from our sin and are therefore equal and have no cause for division. All "enmity," as Paul called it, has been done away with. What was the enmity connected with the Law? It was the

> animosity between believing Jews and Gentiles. . . .
> Jews and Gentiles were enemies because the former
> sought to keep the Law with its commandments and
> regulations (cf. Col. 2:14, 21–23), whereas Gentiles
> were unconcerned about them. This difference was
> like a barrier between them. But now that the Law
> is inoperative ("Christ is the end of the Law"
> [Rom. 10:4]), Jewish-Gentile hostility is gone.[5]

Having united Jews and Gentiles, Christ also reconciled them together to God through the Cross. Christ's death put to death the barrier that separated people from each other and from God. As a result, on the horizontal and vertical planes, Christ has made us one. How thankful we are!

Two Closing Questions

A lesson like this presents several challenges. Let's address the two most significant ones by asking two questions.

First, *do you really believe what you've just read?* Our experiences often lead us to doubt what Paul taught. We see division and alienation all around us. Our churches often segregate along ethnic lines, with racial tensions simmering under the surface—just as they do in the world. If we truly believe what we've read, though, we'll strive to show our unity by treating one another with acceptance, respect, and grace.

Second, *will you really live what you've just learned?* In place of the enmity and dividing wall, Christ laid a foundation for His kingdom of love and peace. He wants to build that kingdom in us and through us as we share His plan of reconciliation and unity with others. Won't you share that message with the people you know? It's a message the world longs to hear.

---

5. Hoehner, "Ephesians," p. 626.

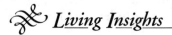 *Living Insights*

In the early 1960s, many were shocked by the controversial book *Black Like Me*. Written by John Howard Griffin, a white man who passed for black by shaving his hair and changing his skin color through a series of medical treatments, the book uncovered what it was like to walk, hitchhike, and ride buses as an African-American through the Deep South. During his travels, he found that people who would normally have been gracious and hospitable toward him instead turned on him with insults and raw hatred.

Sadly, prejudice did not die out in the sixties. It's alive and alarmingly well today—even in our churches.

Though we don't like to admit it, we also look down on others and treat them differently—not only for their skin color or nationality but also for their hairstyles, clothing, and political views. People from different generations may seem odd or even scary to us.

The Bible, as we've seen, lays out a very different plan for God's people. God desires us to live in harmony with one another as a loving family.

In order to make that unity happen in your corner of the world, take some time to examine your life. What prejudices might be lurking in the hidden coves of your heart and mind? What might you do to root them out?

One common indicator of prejudice is stereotyping. What groups do you tend to stereotype, even if your intentions seem harmless?

How do stereotypes dehumanize people?

How do you feel when a stereotype is imposed on a group to which you belong, even when it's not true of you? What about when it *is* true of you?

_____

_____

_____

_____

_____

Fortunately, God's forgiveness also covers prejudice. If you have found this sin in your heart, confess it to Him and ask Him to show you how to tear down walls and build bridges as our Master Builder did.

Chapter 9

GOD'S HOUSEHOLD

Ephesians 2:17–22

As the psalmist wrote, "How good and how pleasant it is For brothers to dwell together in unity!" (Ps. 133:1). And how sad it is when they don't.

There's a story about two brothers who, for forty years, lived in happy harmony as they farmed the same land, built their homes on the same acreage, shared a big, open backyard, and raised their families together. Then something came between them. The older brother would not even speak to his younger brother, the families stayed away from each other, and a grim silence replaced the easy laughter they'd known for so many years.

One day, a handyman came by looking for work. He stopped at the younger brother's house first, and that brother got an angry idea.

"Yes, I sure do have a job for you! See where that creek divides the land? That used to be one green meadow—one parcel of land that was both of ours. But my brother, the stubborn old coot who lives just over there, bulldozed the river levee and put that creek between us. So here's what I want you to do. Take that stack of wood by the barn and go over by the creek and build a fence. Make it good and tall, eight feet high, with no gate. I'll show him that I want to see him even less than he wants to see me! Got it?"

The handyman replied, "Yep, I got the idea. I know what to do."

The younger brother and his family left for a few days to visit his wife's elderly mother. When he came back, the first thing on his mind was to see his fence, so he hurried around back. But what he saw stunned him. Instead of a fence, the handyman had built a wide bridge over the creek that his older brother had made. And who should be coming over that bridge but his brother!

"What a great idea!" the older brother told him, smiling. "It was stupid of me to cut this creek between us. Let's let bygones be bygones and be friends from here on out." The younger brother had enough sense to not tell him that the bridge wasn't his idea. He embraced his brother instead, and they were reconciled.

Afterward, the younger brother turned to the handyman and asked him to stay on awhile to do some other chores. But the handyman replied, "Sorry, can't do it. I've got a lot more bridges

70

to build for other folks!"[1]

In a much greater way, Jesus, too, is a bridge builder—He turned the dividing fence between Jews and Gentiles into a uniting bridge. In fact, Jesus Himself *is* our bridge! Through His death and Resurrection, He has reconciled us to each other, and He has reconciled us all to God. As Eugene Peterson observes, "Jesus, the Messiah, is eternally and tirelessly bringing everything and everyone together. . . . The energy of reconciliation is the dynamo at the heart of the universe."[2]

Christ wants us to do even more than cross the bridge; He wants us to live in the same household, to become a living temple for the glory of our Father. So let's join Paul now in his explanation of the marvelous truth of our new unity in Christ, which indeed is a good and pleasant place to dwell.

Four Changes for God's Household

As Paul continued to explain the new unity we have in Christ, he identified ways in which God's people would change as a result of Christ's breaking down the dividing wall of spiritual and cultural alienation. Paul centered all of these changes on one core truth: *reconciliation*.

As we saw in our previous chapter, reconciliation can transform lives. It can repair years, decades, or even centuries of bitter conflict and restore wholeness. It can occur between individuals or whole nations. Paul affirmed to the believing Gentiles in the Ephesian church that in Christ, reconciliation had already been made.

How did Jesus reconcile God's chosen community (the Jews) with those outside of it (the Gentiles)? Through His Crucifixion and Resurrection, He declared peace, a cessation of hostilities. On the cross, Jesus put to death the enmity between the two, proclaiming that it had come to an end:

> And He came and preached peace to you who were
> far away [Gentiles], and peace to those who were
> near [Jews]. (Eph. 2:17)

---

1. Source unknown.

2. Eugene H. Peterson, *The Message: The New Testament in Contemporary English* (Colorado Springs, Colo.: NavPress, 1993), p. 401.

In addition to being reconciled with each other, both groups—meaning all who believe in Christ—have become one new humanity at peace with God. What does this peace look like? Paul gave us four pictures.

A Common Access to God

First, this new peace reveals itself in *equal and common access to God* by all who believe:

> For through Him we both have our access in one
> Spirit to the Father. (v. 18)

This may not seem like an important development for those of us today who have known common access for nearly two thousand years, but it was a huge change in Paul's day. Jews could access God only through their high priest, who entered God's presence once a year on the Day of Atonement (see Lev. 16). The Gentiles had no access to God at all.

Jesus, however, changed all that when His death tore the temple curtain in two, from top to bottom (Matt. 27:50–51). Now all believers have equal "access" to God—no curtain of separation blocks the way. Paul's particular choice of the word *access* is significant, as New Testament scholar Harold W. Hoehner explains:

> Access can mean "introduction" in the sense that Christ *is* a believer's "introduction" to the Father. But it seems better to understand that Christ *gives* believers access. . . . As so often in this book the work of the Trinity is seen. Here believers have access to God the Father through the Holy Spirit because of Christ's death on the cross.[3]

Paul used this word again in Ephesians 3:12, when he said that because of Christ, "we have boldness and confident access through faith in Him." We can come freely and directly to God in prayer for all our needs—no more priests, no more dividing walls. Instead, we have a common access to God's presence that is total and complete, given to all who believe!

3. Harold W. Hoehner, "Ephesians," in *The Bible Knowledge Commentary*, New Testament edition, ed. John F. Walvoord and Roy B. Zuck (Colorado Springs, Colo.: Chariot Victor Publishing, 1983), p. 626.

A Common Citizenship

Second, Paul explained that the new unity conferred a common citizenship:

> So then you are no longer strangers and aliens, but you are fellow citizens with the saints. (2:19a)

The Gentiles were "strangers" and "aliens"—words that described people who came from foreign countries and held no rights of citizenship in their new nation. But through Christ, the Gentiles became "fellow citizens with the saints"—they were granted the same rights as Abraham, Moses, Joshua, David, Elijah, and every faithful follower of the Lord throughout time. The Gentiles belonged to God's kingdom, and this kingdom was so much more enduring and meaningful than any earthly state they might belong to.

> When Paul wrote these words the kingdom of Rome was at the height of its territorial expansion and glory. Rome dominated the world. Roman armies kept peace and dispensed justice. Roman roads linked the far-flung reaches of the Empire. Rome had stood for hundreds of years and was thought to be able to stand for thousands of years more. But Paul looked at Rome and saw it, not as one great united Kingdom, but as a force imposed on mutually antagonistic factions: rich and poor, free man and slave, man and woman, Jew and Gentile. And in its place he saw this new humanity, created by God himself, transcending these boundaries. This kingdom was destined to grow and permeate all nations, drawing from all peoples. It is a kingdom that cannot be shaken or destroyed.[4]

Our citizenship in God's kingdom, which has been bestowed because of what Christ has done for us, does not result in outward conformity but inward transformation. Like a stained-glass window, we come together with others to let Christ's light filter through us and shine into the world. As we learn to more fully live out our citizenship, we realize that we are part of a people who will endure forever.

---

4. James Montgomery Boice, *Ephesians: An Expositional Commentary* (Grand Rapids, Mich.: Baker Books, 1997), p. 90. Used by permission.

A Common Family

Third, we also relate to each other as a family:

> And [you, the Gentiles] are of God's household.
> (v. 19b)

Family ties are intimate, and the bonds are tight. As God's people, we relate to each other as brothers and sisters and to our Lord as children to a loving father.

This family atmosphere brings with it inestimable privileges and benefits. For one, it provides us with a support network made up of our spiritual brothers and sisters that goes beyond the help of mere friends or neighbors. It also gives us intimacy with our Lord, which means that we can come to Him in prayer at any moment of any day with any need or request with the assurance that He will listen and respond with mercy and grace.

A Common Faith

Finally, we have a common faith, which Paul revealed by using the image of a temple building:

> Having been built on the foundation of the apostles and prophets, Christ Jesus Himself being the corner stone, in whom the whole building, being fitted together, is growing into a holy temple in the Lord, in whom you also are being built together into a dwelling of God in the Spirit. (vv. 20–22)

We're being "built together" as a temple for God! It's important to note several special features of this building. Our foundation is the apostles and prophets. Their teachings—the New Testament Scriptures—form the basis on which we build our lives and our churches. They are lined up with the Lord Jesus, the cornerstone, which is a rich image:

> In ancient building practices "the chief cornerstone" was carefully placed. It was crucial because the entire building was lined up with it. The church's foundation, that is, the apostles and prophets, needed to be correctly aligned with Christ. All other believers are built on that foundation, measuring their lives with Christ.[5]

5. Hoehner, "Ephesians," p. 627.

74

In essence, Jesus Christ Himself sets the direction and forms the basis of the whole family of God. And we are "fitted together" on and in Him with other believers; we're designed to fit tightly together in a living, continually growing "temple" that glorifies God.

What does all this commonality—of access, citizenship, family, and faith—mean to us today? How should we live out the reality of it in our daily lives? Commentator James Montgomery Boice gives us wise counsel:

> If you are in Christ, then in God's sight you are one with every other believer—whether Jew or Gentile, male or female, bond or free—regardless of any distinction whatever. Therefore, you must act like that. You may not see eye to eye with every other Christian on everything. No one expects you to. But you must not break with them! And you must realize that regardless of your differences of opinion, the unity that you have with them is greater than the unity you will ever have with anyone else in the world, even if the unbeliever is of the same class, race, nationality, sex (or whatever) as you are.
>
> Your duty is to live in harmony with these brothers and sisters in Christ, and to let the world know that you are members of one spiritual family. That in itself should be a large portion of your witness.[6]

Three Questions for Members of God's Household

The peace Christ secured for us has opened up a new and glorious spiritual reality. But since we can't see it or touch it, we may miss opportunities to take full advantage of it. Let's ask ourselves three questions that can bring us closer to what is ours in Christ.

First, *do you really believe this?* Yes, we faced this question in our previous chapter, but it's crucial that we come to terms with it. Do you believe Christ has made peace between you and the Father and between you and other Christians?

Second, *have you received it?* Have you accepted that you have access to the Father? That you can approach Him in confidence? That you can freely go to Him in prayer?

6. Boice, *Ephesians*, p. 87. Used by permission.

Third, *are you living like it?* Are you building on the foundation Christ has laid? Are you doing the hard things like making peace with people with whom you've had conflicts?

What privileges are ours: access to God, citizenship in His kingdom, membership in His family, and being living stones in His temple! Yet with these privileges comes the responsibility to take advantage of Christ's breaking down the dividing wall and to live with other believers in harmony and love. This is what it means to be a part of God's household.

〰️ *Living Insights*

Rita Snowden tells the story of man who acquired a "household" mentality:

> In France some soldiers with their sergeant brought the body of a dead comrade to a French cemetery to have him buried. The priest told them gently that he was bound to ask if their comrade had been a baptized adherent of the Roman Catholic Church. They said that they did not know. The priest said that he was very sorry but in that case he could not permit burial in his churchyard. So the soldiers took their comrade sadly and buried him just outside the fence. The next day they came back to see that the grave was all right and to their astonishment could not find it. Search as they might they could find no trace of the freshly dug soil. As they were about to leave in bewilderment the priest came up. He told them that his heart had been troubled because of his refusal to allow their dead comrade to be buried in the churchyard; so, early in the morning, he had risen from his bed and with his own hands *had moved the fence* to include the body of the soldier who had died for France.[7]

Too often we, like the priest, impose false criteria on people before admitting them through our church doors. Sadly, it's often

7. William Barclay, *The Letters to the Galatians and Ephesians*, rev. ed., The Daily Study Bible Series (Philadelphia, Pa.: Westminster Press, 1976), p. 115.

the hurting, needy, and dying whom we turn away. Is there anyone you would bar from your church pews if you had the power (members of other denominations, street people, homosexuals searching for the truth)?

_____

_____

_____

The priest developed a "household" mentality when he discovered a principle that superseded his criteria. What principles do you find in Ephesians 2:17–22 that supercede our human criteria for barring people from God?

_____

_____

_____

Does Paul's principle of unity compel you to "move the fence" for anyone you know or to encourage someone else to "move the fence"? Why or why not?

_____

_____

_____

Paul tells us that the only criteria for becoming a member of God's household is faith in Jesus Christ (Eph. 2:8). Anything we add to that criteria is unnecessary and unacceptable. Let's work to remove those false standards so that we can build God's temple true to the Architect's original design.

Chapter 10

THE MYSTERY, THE MINISTRY, AND ME

Ephesians 3:1–13

I t's unfortunate that we have a chapter break between Ephesians 2 and 3, because the thoughts in these chapters are so closely connected.

Paul was excited about Christ's work of reconciliation between Jew and Gentile and between humanity and God, and he wanted his Gentile readers to take firm hold of their new standing. A passionate prayer for them welled up in his heart (Eph. 3:14–21), but before he could give voice to his feelings, he wanted to tell them more about their reconciliation and how he became a minister of it.

Typical of Paul, he didn't trot out an impeccable résumé. He instead noted his prisoner status and then drew his readers' attention to the most important place: God's grace.

Paul, the Prisoner of Christ

In chapter 3, Paul started to say this:

> For this reason I, Paul, the prisoner of Christ Jesus for the sake of you Gentiles . . . bow my knees before the Father, from whom every family in heaven and on earth derives its name. (vv. 1, 14–15)

Since the Gentiles were now also full members of "God's household" (2:19)—God's own family—Paul wanted to go to their common Father, who gave them their common family name (3:14–15). However, he didn't arrive at this destination by the most direct route. Another important issue sprang to mind and took him down a different avenue of thought. Verses 2–13, then, are a digression, but they are by no means idle rambling. They are about the great mystery of God that Paul was commissioned to declare. And this very commission, this God-ordained call, was what put Paul into prison.

Remember, when Paul wrote this letter, he was under house arrest in Rome (Acts 28). Why was he there? For taking the Good News of God's salvation to the Gentiles. If you read Acts 20–28, you'll find that every time Paul proclaimed that God's salvation had come to the Gentiles as well as the Jews, he was met by a welter of opposition (see Acts 22:21–22; 26:22–24; 28:28–29). What provoked such a hostile response?

First, Paul's message struck at the heart of the Jews' sense of *spiritual privilege. They* were God's chosen ones. *They* were the recipients of His Law. *They* were the ones through whom God communicated to the world. *They* were His children, not the "unclean" Gentiles. Should *they* be one with *them?* Impossible! And second, this sense of spiritual privilege spilled over into a feeling of *racial superiority.* Bigotry injected its poison into their already prideful hearts.

Was God's message stopped by Paul's imprisonment? Not at all! While in prison, Paul wrote four letters that continue to shape our lives today: Ephesians, Philippians, Colossians, and Philemon. God worked through Paul's imprisonment for good (see Rom. 8:28). Remember, nothing touches us that has not first passed through God's hands. God controlled everything in Paul's life, as Acts 23:11 makes clear:

> On the night immediately following [the Sanhedrin's uproar], the Lord stood at his side and said, "Take courage; for as you have solemnly witnessed to My cause at Jerusalem, so you must witness at Rome also."

The Lord's gospel of grace would spread even further—to Jew and Gentile in every realm.

Let's join Paul in Ephesians 3, then, to learn more about the message and ministry that put him in jail—the message and ministry of the gracious gift of God.

The Revelation of the Mystery

Paul called his ministry to the Gentiles "the stewardship of God's grace which was given to me for you" (v. 2). God entrusted him with the message of His grace, which he was to make known to the Gentiles. How did Paul come to know of God's plan?

> By revelation there was made known to me the *mystery,* as I wrote before in brief. (v. 3, emphasis added)

In referring to what he wrote previously, Paul may have been talking about Ephesians 2 or specifically 1:9, where he also used the word *mystery.* This word *mystery* is an important one because it is used three times in Ephesians 3 and six times in the whole letter. What does it mean? John Stott gives us some insight:

> We need to realize that the English and Greek words do not have the same meaning. In English a "mystery" is something dark, obscure, secret, puzzling. What is "mysterious" is inexplicable, even incomprehensible. The Greek word *mystērion* is different, however. Although still a "secret," it is no longer closely guarded but open. . . . The Christian "mysteries" are truths which, although beyond human discovery, have been revealed by God and so now belong openly to the whole church.[1]

What was the mystery about? It was the "mystery of Christ" (v. 4), into which he and the other apostles and prophets were given insight from God (v. 5). Previous generations had been told of a coming Messiah, but they had assumed He would be a Messiah for the Jews. What a surprise it was (and an unwelcome one for many), then, to see this mystery of God's grace unfold as a Jew-Gentile union in Paul's message:

> To be specific, that the Gentiles are *fellow* heirs and *fellow* members of the body, and *fellow* partakers of the promise in Christ Jesus through the gospel. (v. 6, emphasis added)

The Jews of that time thought the Gentiles would "stream" to the mountain of the Lord to learn His ways (Isa. 2:1–4). But the gospel of God's grace proclaimed that through Christ, the Gentiles wouldn't simply admire the Lord and His people from a distance— they would *be* His people too! Paul repeated *fellow* three times to emphasize the equal footing Gentiles have with Jews through Christ. Human birth may bring racial distinctions, but supernatural birth erases them. What a beautiful mystery! What a wondrous grace!

The Declaration of the Mystery

Did the Lord choose Paul to be a steward of His message because

1. John R. W. Stott, *The Message of Ephesians: God's New Society*, The Bible Speaks Today Series (Downers Grove, Ill.: InterVarsity Press, 1979), p. 116. Used by permission of InterVarsity Press-US and InterVarsity Press-UK.

of his superior qualifications? Not according to the apostle, whose words again draw our eyes to God's grace.

Made a Minister by God

> Of [this mystery of Christ] I was made a minister, according to the gift of God's grace which was given to me according to the working of His power. (Eph. 3:7)

Notice, Paul did not make himself a minister; he did not choose to become one through an act of his will. No, it was God's gift—God's grace—that made Paul a minister,[2] through God's miraculous power—the same power that raised Christ from the dead (see 1:19–20)! From his next words, Paul may have been thinking of how God had brought him out of the darkness of spiritual death into the life-giving light of Christ.

Unworthy of the Calling

> To me, the very least of all saints, this grace was given, to preach to the Gentiles the unfathomable riches of Christ. (3:8)

Why would Paul call himself "the very least of all saints"? Because of his past persecution of Christians. He told the Corinthians, "For I am the least of the apostles, and not fit to be called an apostle, because I persecuted the church of God" (1 Cor. 15:9). And to Timothy he wrote, "I was formerly a blasphemer and a persecutor and a violent aggressor. . . . Christ Jesus came into the world to save sinners, among whom I am foremost of all" (1 Tim. 1:13a, 15b). Why did he say these things? To garner pity? To exaggerate his humility? No, he wrote these things about himself to point, once again, to God's grace:

> But by the grace of God I am what I am, and His grace toward me did not prove vain; but I labored even more than all of them, yet not I, but the grace of God with me. (1 Cor. 15:10)

2. In Greek, "Paul *became* (literally, 'was made' or 'created') *a servant* of this gospel. (The word for 'minister,' *diakonos*, refers to a servant but one who held that office in the church. This is different from the word *doulos* meaning 'slave.')" Bruce B. Barton, Philip Comfort, Kent Keller, Linda K. Taylor, and Dave Veerman, *Ephesians*, Life Application Bible Commentary Series (Wheaton, Ill.: Tyndale House Publishers, 1996), p. 63.

Yet for this reason I found mercy, so that in me as the foremost [of sinners], Jesus Christ might demonstrate His perfect patience as an example for those who would believe in Him for eternal life. (1 Tim. 1:16)

As in his other letters, Paul's intent was the same in Ephesians. He, the "very least of all saints," was given by God the grace to preach the gospel to the Gentiles. He would even share the "unfathomable riches" of salvation in Christ—infinite treasure beyond our capacity to understand (Eph. 3:8; see chap. 1).

To Bring to Light God's Wisdom

Also, God assigned Paul

> to bring to light what is the administration of the mystery which for ages has been hidden in God who created all things; so that the manifold wisdom of God might now be made known through the church to the rulers and the authorities in the heavenly places. (3:9–10)

Just as Paul was entrusted with the "stewardship of God's grace" (v. 2), so the church is entrusted with fleshing out the mystery of our unity in Christ. This was one of the messages Paul was to bring to light. "God's whole purpose in Paul's preaching, teaching, and praying ministry is that *the church* should be built up to become the manifestation of God's richly variegated (the word used originally meant 'multi-coloured') wisdom to the *rulers and authorities in the heavenly realms.*"[3]

As if proclaiming God's Good News to the whole world was not enough, Paul's ministry of reconciliation through Christ also impacted another world—the spiritual realm. What does this mean? New Testament scholar Max Turner illuminates this truth for us:

> The rulers in question are probably the whole host of heavenly beings; not merely God's angels nor merely the evil powers of 6:12 but both. They are the assembled witnesses before whom God vindicates his wisdom. He does this through a church

---

3. Max Turner, "Ephesians," in *New Bible Commentary: 21st Century Edition*, 4th ed., rev., gen. ed. D. A. Carson, R. T. France, J. A. Motyer, and G. J. Wenham (Downers Grove, Ill.: InterVarsity Press, 1994), p. 1234.

which brings his wisdom to expression. That wisdom is his eternal purpose in Christ (11), which quite clearly is none other than his intent to unify all things in Christ (1:9–10). It is brought to expression in a universal church where Jew and Gentile live and worship as one body, in harmony with God and with brothers and sisters in Christ (cf. 6; 2:11–22). . . . In this [Paul] follows Jesus whose whole final testamentary prayer in Jn. 17 focused on the request that God keep the church in a unity of love which matches and witnesses to the unity of love between the Father and the Son.[4]

One commentator notes that "the history of the Christian church becomes a graduate school for angels"![5] What an awesome calling—to testify to God's great wisdom in redeeming and reuniting His world through Christ's love. To have a part in such a divine purpose cannot help but motivate us to fulfill His vision of unity.

Encouragement from the Minister

Paul, this prisoner for Christ's sake, concludes his priceless digression by focusing on Christ and encouraging his fellow Christians:

This was in accordance with the eternal purpose which He carried out in Christ Jesus our Lord. (v. 11)

In other words, *the message of the church has eternal roots*. Before Adam and Eve, before the animals, before the plants, before there was light, God planned to bring about salvation and unity through Christ. The Father planned it, the Son implemented it, and the Spirit empowered it. The triune God planned from the beginning of time to proclaim this message through Christ's church. That's awesome, isn't it? But Paul topped even that in the next verse:

In [Christ Jesus] we have boldness and confident access through faith in Him. (v. 12)

We could say that *because our roots are in Christ, we have a secure*

---

4. Turner, "Ephesians," p. 1234.

5. Stott, as quoting Mackay, *The Message of Ephesians*, p. 124. Used by permission of InterVarsity Press-US and InterVarsity Press-UK.

relationship with the Father. What an encouragement this must have been for Paul and his readers! And what an encouragement this can be for us. No suffering, no hardship, no problem can overcome us if we'll remember that we can enter God's presence freely and with joyful trust—we can ask for His help and have confidence that He will give it.

Finally, because of all that God was doing through him for the Ephesians, Paul urged them:

> Therefore I ask you not to lose heart at my tribulations on your behalf, for they are your glory. (v. 13)

In effect, Paul told them, "My being in prison is your glory!" How could this be? It was true because he was imprisoned as a result of fulfilling God's calling for him. Paul, "a Jew, had devoted his life to bringing the Gentiles that gospel, and thought it worth any risk to foster their unity with the Jewish church."[6] If he had not brought the Good News to them, they would still have been living in spiritual darkness, as strangers and aliens without hope, rather than fellow heirs, members, and partakers in Christ's unfathomable riches.

To the Ephesians, Paul's being under arrest may have made the outlook seem bleak, but the *uplook* was clear. God hadn't lost sight of Paul. And He doesn't lose sight of us either. *Our relationship with Him, then, can help guard us from discouragement.*

Aren't we glad Paul followed his train of thought! By grace, Paul made known God's grace to the Gentiles; by grace, Christ made Jew and Gentile one in His church; and by grace, we, Christ's church, proclaim the riches of God's grace to each new generation. In our next chapter, we'll see the natural response to such Good News—to fall on our knees in a prayer of gratitude and awe, as Paul, the prisoner for Christ's sake, did.

❧ *Living Insights*

Before an orchestra can play as one, each musician must tune his or her individual instrument. If you've ever attended a symphony and happened to arrive a few minutes early, you've heard the discordant noise of this tuning period. Without this noise, however, the

---

6. Turner, "Ephesians," p. 1235.

music of the composition would never be as beautiful as it could be.

In many ways, the church is like an orchestra. We're a diverse yet integrated body meant to produce the beautiful sound of the gospel. Too often, however, we're out of tune with each other, sounding more like an orchestra that never took the time to tune up.

Why is this so? Because our congregations are filled with relationships that are not at peace. We've allowed divisive attitudes to go unchecked, and bitterness and resentment have built up.

Do you need to do some tuning up? Is there someone with whom you need to sit down for a talk, for example, either asking for forgiveness or being honest about how he or she has hurt you?

_____

_____

_____

Based on the fact that God's eternal purpose places a high premium on unity, what should be your goal in approaching this person?

_____

_____

_____

Knowing that reconciliation is your goal, how will you talk to this person? What will your tone of voice be? What will you say? What will you try to achieve?

_____

_____

_____

_____

Remember, it's not solely your responsibility to ensure the unity of the body. You can't control what other people in your church choose to do and say; only God can change another person's heart. But by emulating Christ in both your attitudes and actions, you fulfill God's vision for His church.

Chapter 11

PAUL ON HIS KNEES...
AGAIN
Ephesians 3:14–21

ave you ever watched a sunset so stunningly red and orange and purple and gold that you longed to be part of it—to fly into it forever on seagulls' white wings? Or have you ever heard music so poignant and sweet that it made your heart ache—made you long to hear fully the eternal music that distantly echoes in your soul?

There's a yearning in every bit of beauty because we sense that it's only a hint of a larger reality, only the faintest suspicion of God's divine splendor. The greatness of God is higher than our words can reach, farther than our imaginations can stretch, vaster than our hearts can encompass.

Even Paul, a poet-apostle if there ever was one, strained to express God's greatness in a prayer that is deeper than poetry. As we enter Ephesians 3:14–21, it's as if we pass through a portal and step into warm, radiant, color-exploding light. God's power, love, and glory stream out, lifting our hearts to unimaginable heights. Paul's greatest prayer—the crowning prayer of the New Testament—takes us to the heart of God, which is rich toward us beyond our ability to grasp.

Listen as Eugene Peterson peels off the layers of familiarity and renders afresh Paul's soaring wonder and exuberance:

> My response is to get down on my knees before the Father, this magnificent Father who parcels out all heaven and earth. I ask him to strengthen you by his Spirit—not a brute strength but a glorious inner strength—that Christ will live in you as you open the door and invite him in. And I ask him that with both feet planted firmly on love, you'll be able to take in with all Christians the extravagant dimensions of Christ's love. Reach out and experience the breadth! Test its length! Plumb the depths! Rise to the heights! Live full lives, full in the fullness of God.
>
> God can do anything, you know—far more than you could ever imagine or guess or request in your

wildest dreams! He does it not by pushing us around
but by working within us, his Spirit deeply and gen-
tly within us.
Glory to God in the church!
Glory to God in the Messiah, in Jesus!
Glory down all the generations!
Glory through all millennia! Oh, yes![1]
(Eph. 3:14–21 THE MESSAGE)

Let's kneel beside Paul, seeking to more deeply experience God's
extravagant, unimaginable, glorious love.

Prelude

What prompted this prayer, which had been mounting in Paul's
heart for some time? It was the awesomeness of God's mysterious
plan: to reconcile Jew and Gentile to Himself through the grace of
Christ and unite all believers as equals in Himself (see Eph. 2).
This was the "reason" Paul started with in 3:1 and to which he
picked up again in verse 14:

> For this reason I bow my knees before the Father,
> from whom every family in heaven and on earth
> derives its name. (vv. 14–15)

How appropriate to come before the Father, since through
Christ we've been adopted into His family. But how unexpected
for Paul to be on his knees! Unlike our day, when kneeling in prayer
is the norm in many churches, people in Paul's day usually stood
while praying. When they knelt, they did so to show deep adoration,
submissiveness, and urgency.[2] Such was surely the case with Paul,
who not only rejoiced over this new intimacy with the Lord but
also recognized that this Father "ruled the world which owed him
its obedience."[3]

1. Eugene H. Peterson, *The Message: The New Testament in Contemporary English* (Colorado Springs, Colo.: NavPress, 1993), pp. 405–6.

2. See A. Skevington Wood, "Ephesians," in *The Expositor's Bible Commentary*, gen. ed. Frank E. Gaebelein (Grand Rapids, Mich.: Zondervan Publishing House, Regency Reference Library, 1978), vol. 11, p. 50; and Max Turner, "Ephesians," in *New Bible Commentary: 21st Century Edition*, 4th ed., rev., gen. ed. D. A. Carson, R. T. France, J. A. Motyer, and G. J. Wenham (Downers Grove, Ill.: InterVarsity Press, 1994), p. 1235.

3. Turner, "Ephesians," p. 1235.

So this is the setting for Paul's prayer—joyful, awestruck reverence. Let's look more closely at what he asked for the Ephesian branch of God's family . . . and for our branch as well.

Prayer

Paul basically prayed for four things: that we would be strengthened through the Spirit's power, rooted and grounded in Christ's love, able to somehow grasp the immensity of that love, and filled with God's own fullness.

Strengthened through His Spirit

As if spying one gem in a sparkling treasure trove, Paul first picked up the Spirit's strengthening power from the gleaming mountain of God's riches:

> That [the Father] would grant you, according to the riches of His glory, to be strengthened with power through His Spirit in the inner man. (v. 16)

What are "the riches of His glory"? Commentator Charles Hodge tells us that

> it is every thing in God that renders him glorious, the proper object of adoration. The apostle prays that God would deal with his people according to that plenitude of grace and power, which constitutes his glory and makes him to his creatures the source of all good.[4]

Paul prayed that from out of all God's goodness, the Lord would strengthen our inner person—our innermost being made alive in Christ (2:5)—with the Holy Spirit's life-giving power. This "power," interestingly, is the opposite of what happens when we "lose heart" (3:13).[5] Instead of giving in and giving up when times get tough, Paul wanted us to grow in the Spirit's power, to turn more and more to God and His hope. The apostle amplified this thought in verse 17:

> So that Christ may dwell in your hearts through faith. (v. 17a)

4. Charles Hodge, *Commentary on the Epistle to the Ephesians* (1857; reprint, Grand Rapids, Mich.: William B. Eerdmans Publishing Co., 1994), p. 181.

5. See Wood, "Ephesians," p. 51.

As Christians, Christ already lives in our hearts through His Spirit—this happens at the moment of our salvation. What Paul meant by *dwell* was that, through our ever-maturing faith, we would let Christ more and more "be at home in" us—that we would more consistently put (and keep) Christ at the center of our lives, letting Him shape our attitudes and choices and form us into His likeness.[6]

Probably the biggest part of being formed in Christ's likeness is learning to live from a center of love.

Rooted and Grounded in Love

Christ's precious love is the next brilliant jewel Paul picked up:

> And that you, being rooted and grounded in love
> . . . (v. 17b)

What does it mean to be "rooted and grounded" in Jesus' love? The word *rooted* brings to mind plants, with their roots shooting deep into rich earth to be nourished and grow tall and strong. Can you see the tree of Psalm 1, which is "firmly planted by streams of water" (v. 3) and bears fruit and provides shelter? Like that tree, a life rooted in Christ's love also feeds and shelters others—and it, too, is firmly planted and refreshed constantly by God's love for us. The word *grounded* conveys the same idea, but with building imagery—the very foundation of our lives in Christ is love. It's the only thing on earth that can hold the body of Christ together and see us through the tough times.

Comprehending the Immensity of Christ's Love

Paul next prayed that we would be able to somehow "comprehend," or grasp, just how powerful, infinite, and utterly sufficient Christ's love is:

> [That you] may be able to comprehend with all the saints what is the breadth and length and height and depth, and to know the love of Christ which surpasses knowledge. (Eph. 3:18–19a)

As the old hymn goes, "O the deep, deep love of Jesus, Vast,

---

6. See Harold W. Hoehner, "Ephesians," in *The Bible Knowledge Commentary*, New Testament edition, ed. John F. Walvoord and Roy B. Zuck (Colorado Springs, Colo.: Chariot Victor Publishing, 1983), p. 631; and Turner, "Ephesians," p. 1236.

unmeasured, boundless, free!"[7] The love that brought Jesus from heaven to earth to the Cross—for *us*—is limitless:

> Christ's love is total, complete, eternal, and all-encompassing. It reaches every corner of our experience. . . . It is *wide*—covering the breadth of our own experience and reaching out to the whole world. It is *long*—continuing the length of our lives and on into eternity. It is *high*—rising to the heights of our celebration and elation. His love is *deep*—reaching to the depths of discouragement, despair, and even death.[8]

How can we possibly know this love that "surpasses knowledge"? We can't completely. We'll probably spend eternity searching out the vast magnitude of Christ's love. But here's what we can do: We can continually draw our minds back to all that Christ has done for us and why He has done it. We can learn to feel it and rest in the blessed security of it. And we can train our heart's eyes to see His love for others—for "all the saints," with no barriers of race, background, denomination, gender, or age. We can follow the Spirit's tutoring so we love a little more like Christ loves.

Filled with God's Own Fullness

Paul's last request was an amazing one:

> That you may be filled up to all the fullness of God.
> (v. 19b)

No longer are we empty beggars—hungering, weak, alone, in the dark. Because of Christ's immeasurable love, we have the Bread of Life and the resurrection-power of the Spirit (1:19–20). We've been made part of God's family and set in His marvelous light. Paul had prayed that we would be rooted and grounded in this love, that we would somehow comprehend its infinitude, and here he prayed that we would be flooded with it—filled to the capacity of God's own fullness! This certainly does surpass our ability to comprehend, doesn't it?

7. Samuel Trevor Francis, "O the Deep, Deep Love of Jesus," in *The Hymnal for Worship and Celebration* (Waco, Tex.: Word Music, 1986), no. 211.

8. Bruce B. Barton, Philip Comfort, Kent Keller, Linda K. Taylor, and Dave Veerman, *Ephesians*, Life Application Bible Commentary Series (Wheaton, Ill.: Tyndale House Publishers, 1996), p. 68.

Postlude

God's greatness overwhelmed Paul, just as it overwhelms us. So he turned his eyes and ours from ourselves to the One who deserves our worship and all the glory:

> Now to Him who is able to do far more abundantly beyond all that we ask or think, according to the power that works within us, to Him be the glory in the church and in Christ Jesus to all generations forever and ever. Amen. (3:20–21)

This is our God—the One who is so far ahead of us that His works outrun the farthest stretches of our imaginations! The One who does *far . . . more . . . abundantly*—superabundantly! "As the heavens are higher than the earth," He once told us, "So are My ways higher than your ways And My thoughts than your thoughts" (Isa. 55:9). And yet He has chosen to work through *us*, His church, to bring about His new, redeemed society of love.[9]

Praise Him for the mystery of His grace in the church! Praise Him for creating a place where Jews and Gentiles, men and women, rich and poor, and every race and nationality can know unity and harmony! Here alone the miracle of pervasive love erases all hostility and resistance.

Praise Him for the gift of salvation and reconciliation in Christ! Praise Jesus, for He alone has made union and peace between warring parties possible!

Praise Him all people, everywhere, through all time! Just as His gifts are boundless, so are the people He gives them to!

Amen, and Amen!

✣ *Living Insights*

What a great passage Ephesians 3:14–21 is to meditate on and memorize. It encourages and strengthens us no matter what situation we're in, but it's particularly healing when we're discouraged. When we've lost our inner energy and motivation in our walk with Christ, we can remember that He wants to empower us (v. 16; see

---

9. See John R. W. Stott, *The Message of Ephesians: God's New Society*, The Bible Speaks Today Series (Downers Grove, Ill.: InterVarsity Press, 1979), p. 140.

also Isa. 40:28–31). When we lose touch with reality and feel completely unloved and uncared for, He roots and grounds us in His love (Eph. 3:17; see also Jer. 31:3). When our minds are fogged and we don't remember what we once knew so well, He recenters our thoughts on the immensity of His all-embracing love (Eph. 3:18–19a). And when we lose our way with Him and feel empty, He fills us again from the bounty of His presence (v. 19b).

Are you in a time of discouragement now? What's going on?

_____

_____

_____

_____

_____

Are you feeling weak, with no energy for the tasks at hand? If so, have you remembered to pray for God's power to help you? If you haven't, stop right now and ask Him for strength. Write down how He answers your prayer today or in the days to come.

_____

_____

_____

_____

Do you feel unloved and alone in the world? Is your mind fogged over with despair? Recenter yourself in God's love for you by re-reading Ephesians 1–3. Write down the many ways He tells you that you're loved.

_____

_____

_____

_____

_____

_____

_____

Do you feel like you're running on empty? What has brought you to this place? What would you like God to fill you with?

_____

_____

_____

_____

_____

As you end your time of study, take your cue from Paul and focus your mind on the Lord's goodness, spending a while in thankful prayer. Praise the Lord for all He has done and will do, and let Him fill you with His grace, hope, and love!

OUR NEW
Practice
IN THE BODY

Chapter 12

A WORTHY WALK

Ephesians 4:1–6

Most of Paul's letters contain a "hinge"—a point where they shift from theoretical to practical, from principle to application—and Paul signaled this change of direction with the word *therefore* (see, for example, Rom. 12:1; Gal. 5:1; Col. 3:1). As we begin our study in Ephesians 4, the very first word we meet is "therefore" (v. 1 NASB), which is the "hinge" point in this letter.

It's as if we've been lying in cool grass for the past three chapters, watching the stars come out in a soft night sky—there's our adoption as God's own children (1:4–5), there's the hope of our inheritance (1:11, 18), up there is Christ's glorious rule (1:20–23), over there is God's lavish grace (2:1–10), there's our unity with God and each other (2:11–3:13), and all around us is the glow of the Lord's incomparable love (3:14–21).

Now, though, it's time to get up and walk through the gate marked "therefore." On the other side winds a path as far as our eyes can see—the path that takes us home to God, the One who made the stars that light our way. Paul is waiting there, ready to show us how to stay safely on God's path through all the twists and turns that church life, marriage, family relationships, work, and even spiritual battles can bring.

Are you ready to hit the trail? Then let's swing open the gate and learn to walk the path lit by the starlight of God's grace.

How to Walk in Unity

Paul set the tone for the rest of his letter in this first verse of Ephesians 4:

> Therefore I, the prisoner of the Lord, implore you to walk in a manner worthy of the calling with which you have been called.

Once again, Paul drew attention to his being a "prisoner of the Lord." Why? Perhaps he was silently communicating "the level of commitment he expects of himself and of others."[1] His intensity certainly shows in his choice of the word *implore, parakaleo* in the Greek, which can be translated "urge" or "exhort." In other words, he earnestly and urgently wanted the Ephesians to walk "worthy" of their Christian "calling"—a vocation and purpose given by God Himself that shapes every aspect of our lives.

God has called us to a life of holiness—of freedom from sin and transformation into Christ's likeness (see Rom. 6; 8; 1 Pet. 1:13–16). And He has called us to unity—a life that reflects our peace in God and His lordship over all the earth (Eph. 1:20–23; 2:14–18). How do we walk worthy of, or live in a way that honors, this calling? In the next two verses, Paul pointed out several guiding lights to help us find our way:

> With all humility and gentleness, with patience, showing tolerance for one another in love, being diligent to preserve the unity of the Spirit in the bond of peace. (4:2–3)

To gain a better understanding of these qualities and how to live them, let's look at each one individually.

Humility

John Stott notes that humility "is essential to unity."[2] Aside from love, humility most distinguishes us from the rest of the world. Yet it's one of the hardest traits to learn. The Ephesians might have found it particularly difficult because their world despised it.

Humility was not a virtue the Greeks and Romans admired in the least. The picture it drew in their minds was of the abject, servile attitude of a crouching slave.[3] To them, humility marked the absence of self-respect.

Jesus, however, provided a whole new picture, showing that the very Son of God was "gentle and humble in heart" (Matt. 11:29) and had come not "to be served, but to serve" in order to bring us

---

1. Max Turner, "Ephesians," in *New Bible Commentary: 21st Century Edition*, 4th ed., rev., gen. ed. D. A. Carson, R. T. France, J. A. Motyer, and G. J. Wenham (Downers Grove, Ill.: InterVarsity Press, 1994), p. 1236.

2. John R. W. Stott, *The Message of Ephesians: God's New Society*, The Bible Speaks Today Series (Downers Grove, Ill.: InterVarsity Press, 1979), p. 148. Used by permission of Inter-Varsity Press-US and InterVarsity Press-UK.

3. See Stott, *The Message of Ephesians*, p. 148.

salvation (Mark 10:45). Jesus also showed us that humility was to mark His followers' lifestyles when He quietly and gently washed His disciples' feet (John 13:1–17).

In light of Christ's example, how would we define humility? It is *an attitude of the heart that recognizes God's love for and value of others and is willing to put their needs first.* It's the opposite of pride, which turns the spotlight on ourselves and seeks to satisfy the self. In contrast, humility lights up others and seeks to serve with the same dignity and kindness in which Christ Himself chose to live.

Gentleness

Humility and gentleness, or "meekness" (KJV), go hand in hand. Where humility is an attitude, "gentleness is the action derived from it."[4] Contrary to popular belief, meekness is not weakness— it is strength under control.[5]

Gentle people are not harsh with others, don't strive to get their way. Instead, they are considerate and don't complain, bearing "without irritation or resentment the faults and injuries of others."[6] When they get angry, it's usually more at wrongs done to others than wrongs done to themselves.

Gentleness, like humility, is also vital to maintaining unity because it smoothes our rough edges and creates a safe place for everyone. It also reflects Christ's heart, which in His own words is both "humble and gentle" (Matt. 11:29). Jesus even bestowed a special blessing on the gentle, remember? "Blessed are the gentle, for they shall inherit the earth" (5:5).

If all of us in the church balanced our strength with humility and gentleness, as Jesus did, then most of our conflicts would disappear like wisps of smoke dissolving in air.

Patience

Humility may be the hardest of the four traits to learn, but patience comes in the hardest way. Stott gets to the nitty-gritty in his definition: "longsuffering towards aggravating people, such as

---

4. Bruce B. Barton, Philip Comfort, Kent Keller, Linda K. Taylor, and Dave Veerman, *Ephesians*, Life Application Bible Commentary Series (Wheaton, Ill.: Tyndale House Publishers, 1996), p. 74.

5. See Stott, *The Message of Ephesians*, p. 149.

6. Charles Hodge, *Commentary on the Epistle to the Ephesians* (1857; reprint, Grand Rapids, Mich.: William B. Eerdmans Publishing Co., 1994), p. 200.

God in Christ has shown towards us"![7] Patience gives people time—something we all need so much but get and give so little of.

In America today, we are a people who tap our fingers impatiently while the microwave takes all of thirty seconds to heat a hotdog, who practically pull the paper out of the printer because it's not working fast enough, who swerve from lane to lane on the highway to gain a few car lengths on those around us.

But patience is essential, especially in the body of Christ, because it creates an atmosphere of grace that allows us to fail and grow, make mistakes and learn. It clears a space for feelings to cool down and reasonableness to regain its footing. And patience, too, is one of Christ's qualities—He kindly waits for people to repent and receive new life in Him (see Rom. 2:4; 1 Tim. 1:16).

Loving Tolerance

Just as humility and gentleness go hand in hand, so do patience and loving tolerance. Patience makes us gracious, especially when we've been treated poorly. Tolerance is "the action side of patience," which reaches out in forgiveness and empathy.[8]

How can we bring ourselves to empathize, forgive, and treat with grace those who hurt us? By remembering how graciously God has acted toward us. Even when we were dead in our sins—when we were *enemies* of God—He gave us life and lifted us up to heaven to sit with His Son (Eph. 2:5–6; Rom. 5:10). To put a twist on John's words, we can bear with others because God first bore with us (see 1 John 4:19). And we can welcome others with the warm embrace of tolerance because our hearts have been warmed by the flame of God's love.

Diligence in Preserving Unity

Like the last star atop the Big Dipper, diligence in preserving our Christian unity completes Paul's picture of the worthy walk. All of the previous qualities he mentioned—humility, gentleness, patience, loving tolerance—promote our unity as children in God's family. Now we must zealously maintain it, safeguarding it from all the human ills that can tear it apart: selfishness, pride, exclusivity,

---

7. Stott, *The Message of Ephesians*, p. 149. Used by permission of InterVarsity Press-US and InterVarsity Press-UK.

8. Barton and others, *Ephesians*, p. 75.

gossip, favoritism, discord.

Unity (not uniformity, as we'll see in our next chapter) needs to be the persistent and constant concern of every member of Christ's body. Because Christ has established peace (Eph. 2:15)— and Christ *is* our peace (v. 14)—we are called to live in the beautiful "bond of peace" (4:3). In a divisive, warring, wounding world, the most powerful testimony the church can give is genuine unity, prompted by true love and shown in the example of peace. This reflects the reality of God like nothing else on earth.

Why We Walk in Unity

To illustrate the unity God has created in Christ, Paul listed seven of its facets, underscored by the repetition of the word *one* all seven times:

> There is *one* body and *one* Spirit, just as also you were called in *one* hope of your calling; *one* Lord, *one* faith, *one* baptism, *one* God and Father of all who is over all and through all and in all. (vv. 4–6, emphasis added)

Notice, Paul didn't say, "There *will* be . . ." The basis for our unity is not reserved for the future but is real, here and now: "There *is*" . . .

- *One body*—Jews and Gentiles make up a single, harmonious fellowship of believers in a universal church in all ages (see 2:14–16).

- *One Spirit*—the same Spirit of God gives life to and dwells in each of us. He provides a "common principle of life" for us all, and His "presence is the ultimate ground of [our] unity."[9]

- *One hope in our calling*—all Christians share the hope of eternal life in heaven and of being transformed into Christ's sinless likeness. We look forward to a shared future, when Christ will come again and wipe away all our tears—where death, mourning, weeping, and pain fade into dim memories and joy, peace, and unmarred communion with God are ours forever (Rev. 21:4–7, 22–27).

9. Hodge, *Ephesians*, p. 204.

- *One Lord*—Christ rescued us from our futile, sin-enslaved way of life, purchasing us at the high price of His own blood (1 Pet. 1:18–19). We belong only to Him, the One who is the only way to the Father and is one with the Father (John 10:30; 14:6). We're members of His body—He alone is the Head. Christ is the very reason we have come together.

- *One faith*—only belief in Christ's saving work on the cross and in His Resurrection bring us eternal life. Salvation comes only through faith, a faith anchored in the gospel of Jesus Christ. Our shared belief in Christ breaks down all the "dividing walls" of race, nationality, gender, status—and even time.

- *One baptism*—we publicly proclaim our identification with Christ through the unique and unifying sign of baptism, an outward sign of our inner faith. The methods may vary, but we share the meaning of the sign.

- *One God and Father of all*—as God's own children through belief in His Son, Jesus Christ, we all look to one Father. He is the sovereign Creator, the Lord of all who believe. But He's no distant deity, reading the newspaper in His slippers while the world goes spinning by. He is "over all"—sovereignly superintending His creatures and creation. He is "through all"—omnipotently pervading and sustaining us as He works through our lives. And He is "in all"—omnipresently living in us.

Did you notice something? Our unity is founded on the Trinity:

> The one body of believers is vitalized by one *Spirit*, so all believers have one hope. That body is united to its one *Lord* (Christ) by each member's one act of faith, and its identity with Him is depicted by one baptism. One *God*, the Father, is supreme over all, operative through all, and resides in all.[10]

As the Spirit, the Son, and the Father are one, so are we who were created in God's image and re-created to be in Jesus' image (Rom. 8:29; 2 Cor. 3:18). What a glorious reason we have for a worthy walk! After all, if we're going to spend eternity together, why not start living in gracious unity with each other now?

10. Harold W. Hoehner, "Ephesians," in *The Bible Knowledge Commentary*, New Testament edition, ed. John F. Walvoord and Roy B. Zuck (Colorado Springs, Colo.: Chariot Victor Publishing, 1983), p. 633.

Sure, we all have different personalities, different tempera-ments, different gifts, different backgrounds, different convictions, and even different scars. If we let them, these differences can cut across the grain of our expectations, splintering our nerves. But we can also choose to regard them as signals, like flares in the road that tell us, "Slow down. Give some space. Approach with care." A little understanding and freedom go a long way toward creating harmony and unity.

When you think about it, God has called us to a life of great beauty. Peace instead of hostility, grace instead of rigid demands, kindness in place of harshness, enriching companionship instead of lonely striving—all these good and lovely qualities mark the path ahead of us. How could we not want to walk in a manner worthy of the great God who has lavished His love on us with His whole being?

🎍 Living Insights

Here's a riddle for you: What is small but extremely powerful, short in length but long in reach, and can lift up and unite as well as tear down and tear apart?

If you need a little help, Solomon is standing by with some clues—see Proverbs 12:18; 15:4; and 18:21.

Yes, it's that tiny, muscular organ just behind our teeth: the tongue. The words formed and launched by our tongues can wel-come people in or push them away. They reveal the humility, gen-tleness, patience, and tolerant love that wants to keep us safe together in Christ. And they also disclose the pride, roughness, irritability, and judgmental attitudes that wound and fragment the body of Christ.

What do the words spilling over your tongue reveal about you? Take the first quality Paul mentioned, humility. Does what you say affirm God's love and value for other people? Do you consider what someone else may need to hear before you speak your mind? How well does humbleness characterize your speech? What, if anything, would you want to change in this area?

How gentle are your words? Your tone? Do your words create a safe place for others? Or do you tend to launch sharp, flaming arrows that cause others to raise their shields? How well does gentleness mark your speech? How would you like to grow in this aspect?

_____

_____

_____

_____

_____

Do your words give others time and space? Or are words like "Hurry up!" and "Haven't you learned by now?" lurking under your tongue, ready to poison the next child or mistake-prone new believer? How does patience, or the lack of it, come out in what you say to others? How about in what you say to yourself?

_____

_____

_____

_____

Does your tongue easily form words of forgiveness? Or does it stammer over empathy because it's more familiar with anger and rejection? In what ways do your words reveal loving tolerance or its absence?

_____

_____

_____

_____

As with our attitudes and actions, we need to align our words with a God-given purpose: safeguarding the unity Christ created for us on the cross. Now, we won't always agree with each other, and we will hurt and offend and anger each other as we bump along the path toward heaven together. We're still human, remember, which means that things are likely to get quite bumpy! But the *way* we deal with these disagreements and hurts and offenses can make all the difference.

As you reflect on what Paul has taught us and what the Spirit has revealed to you about yourself, remember that we've been united in a "bond of peace" (Eph. 4:3). Let's learn to live more fully in that peace and to speak in a way that upholds it. As James wrote, "The seed whose fruit is righteousness is sown in peace by those who make peace" (James 3:18). May God's peace be the guiding force in your life and in your words.

Chapter 13

His Gift and Our Gifts

Ephesians 4:7–11

Is unity the same as uniformity? Did Paul want us to be cookie-cutter Christians, creating harmony through sameness?

Definitely not! As we pick up in Ephesians 4:7 and read through to verse 11, we'll see that Paul expected a great deal of diversity in the body of Christ. In these verses, his emphasis shifted from discussing what we all have in common to ways that we each complement one another through our unique gifts. Our unity shines through in our *qualities* (character traits, being of the same mind, and the like), while our diversity reveals itself in our *functions* (how we contribute to the body through the variety of spiritual gifts God has given us).

What Christ Did for Us

To use our spiritual gifts effectively, we first need to understand their source of power and how Christ made that power available to us.

He Gave the Gift of Enabling Grace

The source of power behind all spiritual gifts is the Resurrection of Jesus Christ. His power to overcome sin and death is at work in every believer, granting us access to God and enabling us to serve Him effectively. And the switch that activates that power in our lives is God's grace:

> But to each one of us grace was given according to
> the measure of Christ's gift. (v. 7)

Paul used a lesser-known meaning of the word *grace* here, which refers not to our salvation but to the *enabling power* that comes from our salvation. God has given each of us a calling (Christ's gift) and the power (grace) to fulfill it. We need both—Christ's gift and His grace—to exercise our individual spiritual gifts.

He Led Captive a Host of Captives

How did the bestowing of this grace-gift take place? As Paul explained, it came through Christ's Ascension:

Therefore it says,
"When He ascended on high,
He led captive a host of captives,
And He gave gifts to men." (v. 8)

Paul was actually quoting Psalm 68 and giving it a new application. In that psalm, David called for God to rescue His people and vindicate them as He had in the past. The Lord had led His people in triumph during the Exodus (v. 7) so that Mount Sinai quaked (v. 8) and the kings of the earth were scattered (vv. 11–14). Then He set Himself up on His holy mountain (vv. 15–17) and received gifts from men (v. 18).

Paul applied this picture to Christ's Ascension because he saw it as a further fulfillment of God's triumph.[1] Christ, too, after the Crucifixion and Resurrection, led His people to freedom and ascended in victory. He also "led captive a host of captives" (Eph. 4:8), signaling His triumph over His spiritual enemies.[2]

Yet Paul seems to have made a change to the psalm. David declared that the Lord "received gifts among men" (Ps. 68:18). Paul, however, said that Christ "gave gifts" (Eph. 4:8). Commentator John Stott sorts this out for us:

> We need to remember that after every conquest in the ancient world there was invariably both a receiving of tribute and a distributing of largesse. What conquerors took from their captives, they gave away to their own people. The spoils were divided, the booty was shared.[3]

So, we could say that David wanted to highlight the Lord's victory over His enemies, while Paul wanted to show the result of Christ's conquest—the distribution of wealth in the form of spiritual gifts.

Let's take a look at the gifts we received from Christ.

---

1. See John R. W. Stott, *The Message of Ephesians: God's New Society*, The Bible Speaks Today Series (Downers Grove, Ill.: InterVarsity Press, 1979), pp. 156–57.

2. See Bruce B. Barton, Philip Comfort, Kent Keller, Linda K. Taylor, and Dave Veerman, *Ephesians*, Life Application Bible Commentary Series (Wheaton, Ill.: Tyndale House Publishers, 1996), p. 80. This saying has one of two meanings: (1) He led the captured ones into their captivity, or (2) He captured the captors. In either case, the meanings imply the same thing—that Christ defeated His enemies.

3. Stott, *The Message of Ephesians*, p. 157. Used by permission of InterVarsity Press-US and InterVarsity Press-UK.

He Gave Spiritual Gifts

Five passages in the New Testament list about twenty gifts God has given us: Romans 12:6–8; 1 Corinthians 12:8–10, 28–30; Ephesians 4:11; and 1 Peter 4:11. Before we go much further, we should probably define "spiritual gift." It is *a supernatural ability Christ gives to His believers that enables them to perform functions in the church with effectiveness and skill.*

These gifts have a specific purpose: to serve and edify Christ's people, the church. They are meant to draw our eyes to Christ, which means we get joy in using them, but He gets the glory.

Here are a few other facts about spiritual gifts:

- Every believer has at least one gift, but almost always more than one (see 1 Cor. 12:7; 14:1).

- Spiritual gifts are given when we're saved and are used to fulfill God's calling for us (see 1 Cor. 14:26b; Eph. 4:12; 1 Pet. 4:11).

- The gifts are varied and fill different roles. Some are more visible than others, but all are equally important (see 1 Cor. 12:12–25).

- All the gifts derive their power from the same source—the triune God (see 1 Cor. 12:4–6)—and they give glory to the One who so lavishly bestows them (1 Pet. 4:11b).

An Important Parenthesis

The mention of Christ's Ascension led Paul into a short parenthetical thought, where he clarified some of the facts surrounding that event:

> (Now this expression, "He ascended," what does it mean except that He also had descended into the lower parts of the earth? He who descended is Himself also He who ascended far above all the heavens, so that He might fill all things.) (Eph. 4:9–10)

What does "He also had descended into the lower parts of the earth" mean? Three interpretations are commonly accepted: (1) it could mean "into the lower parts, that is, the earth itself," in which case the apostle would be referring to Christ's incarnation, His descent from heaven to earth. Or (2) it may mean "into the lower parts that are below the earth," describing Christ's descent into Hades between His death and Resurrection. Or (3) it may be translated "into the lower parts that belong to the earth," referring to His death and burial.[4] Each interpretation has found favor with respected scholars who interpret the Bible literally, and none alter the important orthodox beliefs of the church.

Whatever disagreements scholars may have over verse 9, they all agree on the essential meaning of verse 10, that Christ ascended to the Father and now "[fills] all things." This last phrase is important because it tells us that Christ did not ascend to leave the world. Rather, He ascended so that He might fill the world more completely with His presence.

Remember what Jesus told His disciples on the night before He was crucified?

> "I tell you the truth, it is to your advantage that I
> go away; for if I do not go away, the Helper will not
> come to you; but if I go, I will send Him to you."
> (John 16:7)

Only when Christ returned to the Father could He send His Spirit and His Spirit's gifts. The Ascension, then, is central, which is why Paul took the time to explain it more deeply.

Four of the Gifts Christ Gave

In his letter to the Ephesians, Paul focused on four spiritual gifts. Let's join him and learn how each one helps equip Christ's people.

Apostle

And He gave some as apostles . . . (Eph. 4:11)

The first gift Paul mentioned was that of *apostleship*, which in a general sense referred to "someone who was sent." The term could also have a more specific meaning, designating a messenger sent out by a church, either as a missionary or some other errand-runner. More likely, though, Paul had in mind a distinctive group of men known as the apostles of Christ. This group included the original twelve disciples (including Matthias, who replaced Judas), Paul, James the brother of Jesus, and possibly a few others.[5] All were men who personally saw the risen Christ and were given absolute authority in the founding of the church.

4. Stott, *The Message of Ephesians*, pp. 158–59. Used by permission of InterVarsity Press-US and InterVarsity Press-UK.

5. These "others" may include Barnabas (Acts 14:14), Andronicus and Junias (Rom. 16:7), Apollos (1 Cor. 4:6, 9) and Silas and Timothy (1 Thess. 1:1; 2:6–7).

The men who held the gift and office of apostle built the church; their gift empowered them to go into unchurched areas, preach the gospel, and successfully start congregations. Since their gift was needed only to get the church started, and since the qualifications included personally seeing the risen Christ, the office of apostle has ceased to exist today.

Prophet

And some [He gave] as prophets . . . (v. 11)

Along with the apostles, the prophets formed the foundation of the church (Eph. 2:20), which is why these two gifts are called the "foundational" gifts. Prophets served three vital roles. First, they foretold the future (Acts 11:28; 21:9–11). Second, they more often exhorted, encouraged, and strengthened God's people (Acts 15:32; 1 Cor. 14:29). Third, and most important, they revealed the Word of God when the New Testament Scriptures had not been completed and recorded. Their message came not from thought and study but from direct revelation from the Holy Spirit.

Since we have the complete Word of God now, we no longer need this gift, and it has ceased to exist today as well. Some people have the ability to draw special insight from the Bible and speak powerfully to our day. They may have a type of prophetic gift in this sense, but they don't hold the office of prophet in the New Testament use of the term.

Evangelist

And some [He gave] as evangelists . . . (Eph. 4:11)

In the early church, the evangelists were the traveling ministers, similar to missionaries today. They went to non-Christian regions and preached the gospel, often starting churches or developing those started by apostles (Acts 21:8; 2 Tim. 4:5).

An evangelist is one who possesses a special ability to communicate the gospel, to make it particularly plain and relevant to unbelievers or to help hesitant people take the step of faith.

Just a note—all of us, whether we have this specific gift or not, have the privilege of sharing Christ's gospel with others. While those gifted in evangelism are to lead out in proclaiming the gospel, we all share in realizing the Great Commission (Matt. 28:18–20). So don't leave it to the "experts"! Christ wants to use each of us to spread the message of His love and grace to a hurting world.

We could call evangelists the obstetricians of the church, for they are the ones whom God uses to usher in new life on the largest scale. And the next group of gifted people, the pastor-teachers, we could call the pediatricians, because they work to help new (and old) believers grow.

Pastor-Teacher

> And some [He gave] as pastors and teachers.
> (Eph. 4:11)

The two terms *pastor* and *teacher* are linked grammatically in the Greek text and refer to a single gift,[6] often called *pastor-teacher*. This single gift, however, had two distinct dimensions. On one hand, the pastoral side of the gift empowered its possessors to shepherd their flocks by meeting the day-to-day needs of the congregation—needs such as counseling, comforting, and guiding. On the other hand, it enabled them to feed their sheep through the teaching of the Word. This gift has not changed over time; pastor-teachers today do the same job as their predecessors of two thousand years ago.

As we can see in the description of these various gifts, God desires diversity in the church. Our unity is enhanced by our variety, not threatened by it. So let's foster people's giftedness. Let's take advantage of what God has given us—His gift and our gifts—by faithfully applying them in His service for the building up of His body.

✣ *Living Insights*

Take a short time-out to read the other passages that address spiritual gifts (Rom. 12:6–8; 1 Cor. 12:8–10, 28–30; 1 Pet. 4:10–11). What gifts do you think God may have given you? Perhaps the following list of explanations will help you pinpoint God's special grace to you.[7]

6. See Harold W. Hoehner, "Ephesians," in *The Bible Knowledge Commentary*, New Testament edition, ed. John F. Walvoord and Roy B. Zuck (Colorado Springs, Colo.: Chariot Victor Publishing, 1983), p. 635.

7. Adapted from Kenneth O. Gangel, *Unwrap Your Spiritual Gifts* (Wheaton, Ill.: Scripture Press Publications, Victor Books, 1983). Some of the gifts mentioned by Scripture (apostleship, healing, tongues, interpretation of tongues, miracles, and prophecy) have been omitted from this list because they appear to have ceased, meaning that Christ no longer endows believers with them as He did with believers in the early church.

- *Administration*—the ability to organize people in the church toward a specific goal

- *Discernment*—an uncanny ability to distinguish truth from error or to evaluate spirits to determine if they are from God or Satan

- *Evangelism*—a special ability to communicate the Good News of Jesus Christ to unbelievers or to train others to do so

- *Exhortation*—the ability to effectively challenge and encourage believers to shore up weaknesses and grow in the faith

- *Faith*—an inclination or ability to genuinely trust God when there seems to be no human or natural basis for that trust

- *Giving*—a joyful and eager generosity that gives resources (material and otherwise) without any motives for self-benefit or reciprocation

- *Hospitality*—a cheerful openness to host, shelter, and feed fellow believers at home whenever the need arises

- *Knowledge*—a knack for understanding the meaning of Scripture

- *Leadership*—Having the zeal and communication skills to rally people in the church around a common cause or goal

- *Mercy*—a devoted, freely given compassion for those who are needy and suffering

- *Ministering*—performing any task that benefits others by joyfully meeting their practical or material needs (also called "helps" or "service")

- *Pastoring/Teaching*—a bent toward caring for and protecting fellow believers, and being able to understand the complex teachings of the Bible and explain them in an easily understandable way

- *Wisdom*—the ability to consistently make wise decisions and provide godly insights for problems

Remember, having gifts doesn't mean you'll be perfect at them. We grow in them, learning how to effectively use them over time. Also, not having a certain gift doesn't mean you won't be able to function at all in that area; we're all called to serve and have compassionate mercy for each other.

Underline the gifts you've enjoyed using in the past, and circle the ones you've received positive feedback on. The gifts that are both underlined and circled are most likely yours.

If you're not getting a clear picture of what your gifts might be from this exercise, don't get discouraged. Discovering your gifts is a process that takes both time and effort. The best way to go about finding yours is to (1) experiment with the different gifts (teach a lesson, try your hand at evangelizing, and so on), (2) ask for feedback from people who have witnessed your attempts, and (3) possibly consult a gift-discovery test (listed in the Books for Probing Further section of this guide). Most important, pray about it, asking God for His leading and insight.

As you discover your spiritual gifts, practice using them. Like our bodies' muscles, the more we use them, the stronger they become. Look for opportunities to work out your spiritual gifts, and as you do, you'll find that your service is more fruitful and invigorating than ever before.

Chapter 14

BODY LIFE AT ITS BEST

Ephesians 4:12–16

How much trouble can a little comma cause? A bunch!

Did you know that our English translations of Ephesians contained a misplaced comma clear up until 1903?[1] The error was found in chapter 4, verse 12, the first verse of five we'll be looking at in this study, and here's how it read before the correction was made:

> For the equipping of the saints, for the work of service,
> to the building up of the body of Christ.

That first comma is the troublemaker, between the words *saints* and *for*. It doesn't look too dangerous on the surface, but it has caused a lot of problems over the years. Why? Because it implies that the people listed in verse 11—the apostles, prophets, evangelists, and pastor-teachers—are the ones solely responsible for performing the three functions of the church listed in verse 12, that is, equipping the saints, serving, and building up the body.

Without the comma, however, the verse takes on a completely different meaning, indicating that the ministers listed in verse 11 fulfill the first function—equipping the saints—and that the saints, duly equipped by the ministers, then do the work of service. Both groups, performing their individual functions, fulfill the third function—building up the body.

Read the verse again with its proper quotation:

> For the equipping of the saints for the work of service, to the building up of the body of Christ.

Can you see the difference? The church functions best when the clergy and laity work in partnership toward a common goal. In ages past, however, many professional ministers developed a philosophy of church structure known as *clericalism* that was based on the misplaced comma in Ephesians 4:12 and other misinterpretations

---

1. A commentator named Armitage Robinson finally discovered it. See John R. W. Stott, *The Message of Ephesians: God's New Society*, The Bible Speaks Today Series (Downers Grove, Ill.: InterVarsity Press, 1979), p. 166.

of Scripture. They drew a false distinction between professional ministers and churchgoers and stated that the work of the church was to be done by those paid to do it. Consequently, church officials relegated the lay members to following docilely and, of course, supporting financially the professionals.[2] As a result, power-hungry ministers abused their position in order to amass wealth and prestige, and the growth of the church was severely stunted.

Thank goodness we've since worked out that comma problem! Now we can experience body life at its best in vibrant and growing churches, and all of us can play a significant part in God's plan for the church. To find out what that plan is and how each of us can contribute to it, let's examine verse 12 as it was meant to be read.

Three Reasons for God's Gifts to the Church

As we've already hinted, verse 12 tells us that God had three reasons for giving spiritual gifts to the members of His body. Let's take a look at each reason individually.

For the Equipping of the Saints

God gave professional ministers to the church for the "equipping of the saints." But what does *equipping* mean? The Greek word *katartismos*

> is used in surgery for setting a broken limb or for putting a joint back into its place. In politics it is used for bringing together opposing factions so that government can go on. In the New Testament it is used of mending nets (*Mark* 1:19), and of disciplining an offender until he is fit to take his place again within the fellowship of the Church (*Galatians* 6:1). The basic idea of the word is that of putting a thing into the condition in which it ought to be.[3]

How should a minister carry out this kind of "equipping" of the saints?

---

2. See James Montgomery Boice, *Ephesians: An Expositional Commentary* (Grand Rapids, Mich.: Baker Books, 1997), p. 141.

3. William Barclay, *The Letters to the Galatians and Ephesians*, rev. ed., The Daily Study Bible Series (Philadelphia, Pa.: Westminster Press, 1976), p. 149.

It is the function of the office-bearers of the Church to see that the members of the Church are so educated, so guided, so cared for, so sought out when they go astray, that they become what they ought to be.[4]

With awesome responsibilities like these, it's no wonder that the Chief Shepherd will bestow the "unfading crown of glory" on ministers who faithfully fulfill their calling (1 Pet. 5:1–4).

For the Work of Service

Ministers aren't the only ones called to serve, though. They equip the rest of us so that we can serve in Christ's name too. Otherwise, the church would begin to look like a football game— 50,000 onlookers in the stands desperately in need of exercise, watching twenty-two people on the field desperately in need of rest!

Fortunately, in God's design all of us—not just the "professionals" —have something to contribute. And when we combine our strengths, we can accomplish the tasks at hand.

For the Building Up of the Body

The goal of equipping and serving is the building up of the body. We do this in two ways: first, by caring for and showing love to fellow Christians and exercising our spiritual gifts; and second, by reaching out to our community, meeting people's physical and emotional needs, and sharing Christ's saving love.[5] Both ways strengthen and stretch the body, helping us grow into a closer likeness of Christ Himself.

Four Signs of a Built-Up Body

How can we know if we're fulfilling God's purposes for the church? How can we tell if our local body is as "built up" as it should be?

Mature Minds

The first sign of a grown-up congregation is that the believers

---

4. Barclay, *Galatians and Ephesians*, p. 149.

5. Bruce B. Barton, Philip Comfort, Kent Keller, Linda K. Taylor, and Dave Veerman, *Ephesians*, Life Application Bible Commentary Series (Wheaton, Ill.: Tyndale House Publishers, 1996), p. 83.

possess mature minds:

> Until we all attain to the unity of the faith, and of
> the knowledge of the Son of God, to a mature man,
> to the measure of the stature which belongs to the
> fullness of Christ. (Eph. 4:13)

One of the hallmarks of maturity is the gentle pursuit of unity. Remember Paul's counsel at the beginning of Ephesians 4? He told us to be diligent in preserving our spiritual unity by treating one another with humility, gentleness, patience, tolerance, and love (vv. 2–3). Christ is our peace with God and each other (2:14–16), and we live in His peace by recalling our unity and protecting it.

Yes, unity needs protection—from selfish desires and seeing only our own needs. To safeguard unity, we need to work toward the greater good of others and train ourselves to look beyond the narrow view of our own needs to the needs of Christ's church and the world He wants us to reach. And, as Paul counseled next, we can preserve unity by seeking to know Christ more and more deeply.

"The knowledge of the Son of God" (4:13b) is not only more complete scriptural knowledge but also experiential knowledge that comes through following Christ day by day.[6] Paul himself desired this kind of knowledge, as we see in his letter to the Philippians: "That I may know Him and the power of His resurrection and the fellowship of His sufferings, being conformed to His death" (3:10). He wanted knowledge that went beyond what he could pack into his head, knowledge that would seep into his heart and flow out through his life in the form of obedience and service.

Stability

Maturity, as expressed through unity and knowing Christ, leads to the second sign, spiritual stability:

> As a result, we are no longer to be children, tossed
> here and there by waves and carried about by every
> wind of doctrine, by the trickery of men, by crafti-
> ness in deceitful scheming. (4:14)

Paul often warned congregations in the early church against false teachers. The Ephesian church was no exception. Paul first

---

6. See Boice, *Ephesians*, p. 148.

warned the Ephesian elders of the subtle heresies enticing their flock around A.D. 58 (Acts 20:26–31). This epistle, written in A.D. 61, again cautioned them about false teaching, and then, in A.D. 64 and 66, he even more strongly admonished Timothy who was ministering in Ephesus (1 Tim. 1:3–6; 4:1–2; 6:20–21; 2 Tim. 1:13–14; 2:14–26). Even after Paul, well into the 80s and 90s, the congregation was still fighting heretics (1 John 2:18–19; 4:1–3; Rev. 2:1–7).[7]

These false teachers were deliberate in their deception and evil in their motives. Paul mentioned that they employed "trickery"— referring to the way a gambler might cheat at dice—and "craftiness" —denoting an unscrupulousness that will stop at nothing.[8]

If the Ephesians were like immature children, who are easily deceived and led astray, then they would certainly fall prey to those smooth-talking predators. With mature minds, though, they would have stability. They would stand firm against the Pied-Piper teachers and their sweet-sounding false doctrines.

Truthful Tongues

If one kind of immature believer is like a child, unable to distinguish between doctrinal purity and heresy, another kind is like a lopsided scale, unable to balance a passion for truth with a love for others. True maturity, then, gives us the third sign of a built-up body: speaking the truth in love:

> But speaking the truth in love, we are to grow up
> in all aspects into Him who is the head, even Christ.
> (Eph. 4:15)

"Speaking the truth in love" does not fully translate the verb Paul used, *aletheuontes*, because the English language has no comparable verb. A better rendering might be "truthing in love,"[9] which includes all we think and do, as well as what we say.

Balancing truth and love is often difficult to do. Some of us are good at truth—we can spot the smallest flaw in a person's theological

7. Barton and others, *Ephesians*, p. 85.

8. A. Skevington Wood, "Ephesians," in *The Expositor's Bible Commentary*, gen. ed. Frank E. Gaebelein (Grand Rapids, Mich.: Zondervan Publishing House, Regency Reference Library, 1978), vol. 11, p. 59.

9. Harold W. Hoehner, "Ephesians," in *The Bible Knowledge Commentary*, New Testament edition, ed. John F. Walvoord and Roy B. Zuck (Colorado Springs, Colo.: Chariot Victor Publishing, 1983), p. 635.

wardrobe and have no fear of pointing it out. But in our zeal for preserving the integrity of the Scriptures, we can easily hurt others by failing to show them love.

Others of us have the opposite problem. Desiring to keep peace, we let false teaching go uncontested or allow a lie to go uncorrected. We just can't bring ourselves to tip anyone's boat for fear that we'll cause too many waves in the church.

God wants us to be neither abrasive nor timid. Rather, He wants us to show both strength and love. John Stott fittingly summed up this need for balance:

> Truth becomes hard if it is not softened by love; love becomes soft if it is not strengthened by truth. The apostle calls us to hold the two together.[10]

Cooperation

Finally, a built-up group of believers is known for its cooperation:

> From whom the whole body, being fitted and held together by what every joint supplies, according to the proper working of each individual part, causes the growth of the body for the building up of itself in love. (v. 16)

Just as a body is healthy when all its parts are operating properly and working in unison, so a church is healthy when all its members submit to the headship of Christ, walk in the Spirit, contribute to the congregation with their gifts and talents, and live in harmony with each other. The body grows as the individual members grow, and the members grow as they feed on the Word and minister to one another.

Growth is a process. It takes time. The church doesn't become mature overnight any more than our individual bodies do. But since God is working to build us up, we have to trust Him and be patient as He works. And if we do bear with Him, we'll experience church life as He designed it—body life at its best!

---

10. Stott, *The Message of Ephesians*, p. 172. Used by permission of InterVarsity Press-US and InterVarsity Press-UK.

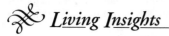 *Living Insights*

A congregation can grow only as much as its individual members grow. Are you willing to commit time and energy to your own development so that you can contribute to the building up of your church? If you are, take the next few minutes to examine how built-up you are in the four areas we discussed in the chapter.

The key to a mature mind is saturating your thoughts with the pure truth of Christ's words. Reflect on the images and messages in your mind lately. Have they been soaking in worry, anger, or fear? What words of our Lord can help you purify those thoughts? (See, for example, Matt. 6:25–34; 11:28–30; Mark 6:45–52; John 10:7–18.)

_____

_____

_____

_____

_____

Have you struggled in the area of stability? Are you able to spot biblical error easily? Has some deceptive teacher ever pulled you off course? What might help you avoid instability in the future?

_____

_____

_____

_____

_____

When it comes to speaking the truth in love, do you tend to overlook untruths for the sake of keeping the peace? Or do you attack it with a vengeance, ignoring love in the process? How did you come to this conclusion? What situations came to mind? What can you do to bring yourself back into balance?

_____

_____

_____

_____

_____

_____

Finally, how well do you cooperate with others in your church? Do you get along well with them, or do you find yourself constantly at odds? Again, identify specific examples. What can you do to contribute to a more cooperative spirit?

_____

_____

_____

_____

_____

_____

As you try to make these improvements, remember that only Christ can bring about lasting change in your life. Only by focusing on and trusting in Him day by day and moment by moment can He transform you into what He wants you to be. And only then can He make His body its best.

Chapter 15

HERE'S HOW TO
GET DRESSED

Ephesians 4:17–24

When it comes to clothing, we've come a long way since Adam and Eve.

Instead of the first pair's "fig-leaves-for-all-occasions" wardrobe, we have a mind-boggling array of shoes, socks, pants, shorts, shirts, blouses, hats, accessories, outer garments, and undergarments from which to choose for any conceivable situation.

With this endless array of choices, how do we determine what to wear? Without exception, we choose our attire based on our purpose. If we want to impress others with our class and sophistication at a gala ball, we don sharp tuxedoes and elegant evening gowns. But if we need to storm a beach or capture an enemy outpost, we would choose something a little more practical—say, military fatigues and combat helmets.

The Christian life is no different. Ephesians tells us that we must wear the right "clothes" for our new lives in Jesus Christ. Paul has outlined our purpose since the beginning of Ephesians: to glorify God by building up His church. But before we can put on our new clothes, we first need to take off our old ones. Thankfully, in 4:17–24, Paul told us how to do both. So let's step into the apostle's changing closet to get fitted for a new set of duds for our new selves.

The Old Wardrobe

Do you remember the tattered and soiled rags of sin you wore before you believed in Christ? For most of us, those memories haven't faded as quickly as we'd like. Sometimes, though, we even keep a set of old clothes in the closet so we can slip back into familiar, comfortable sin patterns every now and then. That's why Paul told us to make a clean break from the past, to throw out *all* of our rags *for good:*

> So this I say, and affirm together with the Lord,
> that you walk no longer just as the Gentiles also
> walk, in the futility of their mind. (4:17)

Paul used the word *Gentiles* to mean those without God's righ-teous Law. He was referring to the old, sinful lives his readers had lived before they placed their trust in Christ. Back then, their thoughts were futile—they had no goal, purpose, or consideration of God.[1] In order to help them reject their old ways, Paul clearly defined what those ways were like.

A Dark Mind

According to Paul, unbelieving people are

> darkened in their understanding, excluded from the
> life of God because of the ignorance that is in them.
> (v. 18a)

"Understanding" and "ignorance" both point to the mind. Why are our minds so important? Because what we think determines the choices we make, which in turn shapes the path of our lives. As the old saying goes, "Where the head leads, the rest will follow."

Unfortunately, unbelievers have "darkened" their minds by blocking out God's light. And they are ignorant of God's ways, having alienated themselves from the Source of true life. They fall headlong into a pit of spiritual death and therefore are "excluded from the life of God." Their disordered, sinful, spiritually dead lives are merely the logical outgrowth of a deeper problem—disordered, sinful, spiritually dead minds.

What a shock wave this statement must have sent through the people of Paul's day. The Greco-Roman society thought the human mind was the best, noblest, and most worthwhile part of the human being—they even considered it divine. They earned salvation by conquering their corrupt, evil flesh with the sword of reason. And with geniuses like Socrates, Plato, and Aristotle to boast of, they took great pride in their intellectual enlightenment.

How offended they must have felt, then, when Paul called their light "darkness" and their salvation "exclusion." No matter how powerful their intellects were, they lacked spiritual perception, and they floundered in the darkness of this world.

Like the Greeks of old, we, too, take pride in our intellects and in our philosophical and technological achievements. And many

---

1. Harold H. Hoehner, "Ephesians," in *The Bible Knowledge Commentary*, New Testament edition, ed. John F. Walvoord and Roy B. Zuck (Colorado Springs, Colo.: Chariot Victor Publishing, 1983), p. 636.

brilliant people today, as in Paul's society, won't accept the simple truth of the gospel. Their minds are agile, but they still need God to "turn the lights on," to illuminate their spiritual minds.

A Hard Heart

Paul directly linked a darkened mind, alienation from God, and erring ignorance to a single root cause—a hard heart:

> Being darkened in their understanding, excluded from the life of God because of the ignorance that is in them, *because of the hardness of their heart.* (v. 18, emphasis added)

The Greek word translated "hardness" is *porosis,* which came from *poros,* meaning "stone." It usually referred to an especially hard kind of marble and could often mean "petrified." This term was also used medically to describe certain calluses and the healing overgrowth that covers fractured bones. Applied to the eyes, it meant blindness.[2] In this case, applied to the heart, *porosis* emphasized how closed off their hearts were from God.

But Paul had an additional nuance of meaning in mind here— *willfulness,* as New Testament scholar Max Turner points out:

> In Scripture ["hardness of heart"] means sheer rebelliousness, not emotional insensitivity. . . . This leads to further darkened understanding as God is displaced from the central position he should occupy. This in turn leads to failure of the human conscience and the downward spiral in sin (v. 19).[3]

The effects of this "failure of the human conscience" are Paul's focus in the next verse.

A Sin-Filled Life

A dark mind, a dead soul, and a hard heart don't exactly produce a garden of delights in a person's life:

---

2. See James Montgomery Boice, *Ephesians: An Expositional Commentary* (Grand Rapids, Mich.: Baker Books, 1997), p. 155.

3. Max Turner, "Ephesians," in *New Bible Commentary: 21st Century Edition,* 4th ed., rev., gen. ed. D. A. Carson, R. T. France, J. A. Motyer, and G. J. Wenham (Downers Grove, Ill.: InterVarsity Press, 1994), p. 1239.

And they, having become callous, have given themselves over to sensuality for the practice of every
kind of impurity with greediness. (v. 19)

Look at these bitter fruits: insensibility . . . lewdness . . .
degradation . . . grasping greed. Poison apples. Two of Paul's terms
are particularly strong: "sensuality," *aselgeia* in the Greek, and
"greediness," *pleonexia*. Commentator William Barclay sheds some
light on these:

> The man who has *aselgeia* in his soul does not care
> how much he shocks public opinion so long as he
> can gratify his desires. Sin can get such a grip of a
> man that he is lost to decency and shame. He is like
> a drug taker who first takes the drug in secret, but
> comes to a stage when he openly pleads for the drug
> on which he has become dependent. . . . A man
> can let his sexual desires so master him that he does
> not care who sees him satisfy them.
>
> . . . *Pleonexia* [is] another terrible word, which
> . . . has been defined as the spirit in which a man
> is always ready to sacrifice his neighbor to his own
> desires. *Pleonexia* is the irresistible desire to have
> what we have no right to possess. It might issue in
> the theft of material things; it might issue in the spirit
> which tramples on other people to get its own way.[4]

What a choking, stinking moral cesspool! "Walk no longer" like
this, Paul said (v. 17). Christ has pulled us out of the muck, cleaned
us, and given us new, beautiful garments to wear.

A Change of Wardrobe

In contrast to futility and darkness, Christ's way is brilliant and
clean and alive. He embodies the truth, which is "divine reality,
light, and life."[5] Done with darkness, Paul wanted the Ephesians
to turn their eyes toward Christ:

> But you did not learn Christ in this way, if indeed

---

4. William Barclay, *The Letters to the Galatians and Ephesians*, rev. ed., The Daily Study Bible
Series (Philadelphia, Pa.: Westminster Press, 1976), p. 153.

5. Turner, "Ephesians," p. 1239.

you have heard Him and have been taught in Him, just as truth is in Jesus, that, in reference to your former manner of life, you lay aside the old self, which is being corrupted in accordance with the lusts of deceit, and that you be renewed in the spirit of your mind. (vv. 20–23)

Cleaning Up with a Renewed Mind

Notice what Paul centered on first: a renewed mind (v. 23). That's a 180-degree difference from the mind mired in futility. How do we renew our minds? We give them a spiritual education. Paul's use of the terms *learn, heard,* and *taught* tell us that he had the image of a school in mind. Let's take a closer look at these three verbs.

First, Paul stated that the Ephesians "learn[ed] Christ." Jesus was the *subject* or substance of their studies. But they did more than learn information about His earthly life, death, and Resurrection; they learned *Him*—His Lordship, His ethics, His kingdom purposes.[6]

They also "heard" Christ, meaning that Jesus was also their *teacher*. Although the words were spoken by Paul, his words came through Christ's Spirit. So the Ephesians had heard the very words of Christ and were actually taught by Him.

Finally, they were "taught in Him." Christ, in addition to being their subject and teacher, was also the very *atmosphere* in which they learned, or, as James Montgomery Boice puts it, Jesus was the school too![7] "Taught in Him" can also convey the idea of being "in communion with him."[8]

With Christ in and above and around us, there's no room left for our old way of life. It yearns for deceit, but our new life in Christ hungers for truth. So Paul told us to remove our old clothes and throw them away—they're decaying with every passing moment anyway (v. 22)—and "be renewed in the spirit of" our minds (v. 23). What does this mean? It means leaving behind values and choices that reject God and His ways and embracing a new mind-set—one that eagerly cooperates with God's will and Christ's way

6. See John R. W. Stott, *The Message of Ephesians: God's New Society,* The Bible Speaks Today Series (Downers Grove, Ill.: InterVarsity Press, 1979), p. 179.

7. See Boice, *Ephesians,* p. 161.

8. Charles Hodge, *Commentary on the Epistle to the Ephesians* (1857; reprint, Grand Rapids, Mich.: William B. Eerdmans Publishing Co., 1994), p. 257.

of life. Renewal goes deeper than changing outer habits; it's an inside job in which we daily admit that our old selves are corrupt and affirm that our new selves are Christlike and extremely fulfilling. It's like taking a shower every day that cleanses and readies us to put on the Christlike clothes of our new wardrobe.

Putting on the Likeness of God

> And put on the new self, which in the likeness of God has been created in righteousness and holiness of the truth. (v. 24)

Just as God created Adam from the dust of the ground, He formed our new selves from the raw material of righteousness, holiness, and truth—qualities that reflect the likeness of our Creator. We aren't shaped by the corrupt lusts of deceit (v. 22) but are formed in purity and justness, the very character of God.

A Final Word

What conclusion can we draw from Paul's words in this passage? Simply that we express our new self in our heart, mind, soul, and behavior. Commentator R. Kent Hughes challenges us to act like the new people we are:

> We have our part to do in dressing ourselves with the divine wardrobe, for here clothes do make the man—and the woman! We must daily set aside the rotting garments of the old man. We must formally reject sensuality and selfish pride and materialism and bitterness. We must read the Word and ask God to renew our minds through the Spirit. We must work out our salvation by doing those things that will develop a Biblical mind. We must put on our new, shining garments of light. We must put on what we are![9]

Christ has revived our hearts with grace and renewed our minds with truth. He's created a new spirit within each one of us. Let's put on new clothes that match!

9. R. Kent Hughes, *Ephesians: The Mystery of the Body of Christ*, Preaching the Word Series (Wheaton, Ill.: Good News Publishers, Crossway Books, 1990), p. 144.

❧ *Living Insights*

One of the most important concepts to learn about the spiritual life is our need to renew the mind. But what, specifically, does that mean? To see how Scripture answers this question, take a look at the verses listed below. Write out in your own words what each one teaches about renewing the mind.

Psalm 1:1–2 _____

_____

_____

Romans 12:1–2 _____

_____

_____

2 Corinthians 10:5 _____

_____

_____

Philippians 1:9–11 _____

_____

_____

Philippians 4:8–9 _____

_____

_____

2 Timothy 3:14–17 _____

_____

_____

Now that you've identified many ways to renew your mind, write out a definition in your own words.

_____

_____

_____

_____

_____

_____

_____

_____

_____

_____

As believers, we can't allow outside influences, such as television, radio, and advertisements, to determine what our minds dwell on. Instead, we must remain ever vigilant to fill ourselves with good and godly thoughts. That is the way of the righteous. It is the way of the new self. It is indispensable to the new wardrobe.

Now that you know how, why not get dressed?

Chapter 16

STEPS THAT LEAD TO FREEDOM
Ephesians 4:25–32

A scan of Paul's epistles reveals how dearly the apostle held our spiritual freedom in Christ:

> For the law of the Spirit of life in Christ Jesus has set you free from the law of sin and of death. (Rom. 8:2)

> Now the Lord is the Spirit, and where the Spirit of the Lord is, there is liberty. (2 Cor. 3:17)

> It was for freedom that Christ set us free; therefore keep standing firm and do not be subject again to a yoke of slavery. (Gal. 5:1)

> For you were called to freedom, brethren; only do not turn your freedom into an opportunity for the flesh, but through love serve one another. (v. 13)

Many of us have experienced the joys of spiritual freedom, walking confidently in the power of the Holy Spirit, but we've also, at times, given up that freedom by giving in to temptation.

What must we do to live in the full measure of freedom God has given to us? As we saw in our previous study, we need to put off the old self and put on the new. In this chapter, Paul's letter reveals five traits of people who wear that new wardrobe. We might even think of these traits as freedom steps—steps that lead to fully experiencing our freedom in Christ.

Living Free

Interestingly, these traits or steps all concern relationships. Holiness happens in the real world, in the church, and in our relationships with others. And notice the way Paul presented them: he balanced negative commands with positive ones, and he explained his reason for the command—connecting our behavior to our beliefs.[1]

---

1. See John R. W. Stott, *The Message of Ephesians: God's New Society*, The Bible Speaks Today Series (Downers Grove, Ill.: InterVarsity Press, 1979), p. 184.

Let's join him as he leads the way along the freedom trail.

Freedom from Falsehood

> Therefore, laying aside falsehood, speak truth each one of you with his neighbor, for we are members of one another. (4:25; see also Zech. 8:16)

The word *falsehood, pseudos* in the Greek, includes all forms of lying, from out-and-out contradictions of truth to carefully-couched counterfeits. Paul may have been referring here to "the great lie of idolatry," as he was prone to do (see Rom. 1:25). Because the Ephesians had renounced the supreme falsehood of paganism, he urged them to take that decision even further by forsaking all "lesser" lies.[2] Likewise, for us to grow as Christians, we, too, need to uproot falsehood and cultivate truthfulness.

While personal spiritual growth is a good reason to live truthfully, Paul added another: "We are members of one another." Lying is a sin against the church—it undermines trust and causes conflicts, tears down relationships and threatens unity. Jesus reminded us that Satan is the father of lies (John 8:44), and when we lie, we're following his ways. But the Lord is a God of truth (Isa. 65:16). As members of His body, eternally joined and related in love, truth is our new birthright and a mark of those who belong to God.

Freedom from Anger

> Be angry, and yet do not sin; do not let the sun go down on your anger, and do not give the devil an opportunity. (Eph. 4:26–27)

Paul's first words, "Be angry, and yet do not sin," echo Psalm 4:4. Does it surprise you that the Bible allows us—in both Testaments— to get angry? Now, Paul and David didn't have in mind temper tantrums but righteous anger that directs its rage at the appropriate object—sin and sinful behavior, not sinners. And it's expressed for the right reason—to defend God's righteous standards, not to avenge personal grievances. Jesus' driving the money-changers from the temple because they had turned God's house into a place of personal profit is a good example of righteous anger (Matt. 21:12–13;

---

2. Stott, *The Message of Ephesians*, pp. 184–85. Used by permission of InterVarsity Press-US and InterVarsity Press-UK.

see also Mark 3:1–5). We could use more of this kind of anger today. Too often we remain silent and apathetic while sin and injustice run roughshod over people.

Unfortunately, we more often become angry because others fail to give us what we want. They may not give us the full measure of respect we feel we deserve, they may inconvenience us, or they may hurt our feelings. Whatever the cause, our anger often stems from selfish desires, not holy vigilance.

So Paul urged the Ephesians—and us—to guard against impure motives and harmful expressions of our anger. In fact, he counseled, "Do not let the sun go down on your anger." Don't brood on it or hold a grudge. Understandably, not all conflicts can be resolved before bedtime; sometimes we may need to take a breather in the process of working matters out. But the key is to continue to move toward resolution so we aren't stuck in our anger.

If we string out our conflicts, then we "give the devil an opportunity" to drive a wedge between us and other believers. And he'll use that wedge to bring divisions into the church, as well as into our personal lives. In contrast, God has designed the path of freedom to be traveled in peace, by a people united and empowered by love.

Freedom from Theft

> He who steals must steal no longer; but rather he must labor, performing with his own hands what is good, so that he will have something to share with one who has need. (Eph. 4:28)

Stealing encompasses a whole array of activities, from the obvious, such as shoplifting, embezzling, and taking office supplies, to the subtle, such as wasting time at work. Whatever the activity, modern or ancient, Paul exhorted his readers to "steal no longer."

Instead, Paul directed us to work. Through the work of our hands, we not only provide for ourselves but contribute to the good of others. Christ created us for good works, remember (2:10)? By generously caring for those in need, we bring His love to others and find joy in fulfilling our calling.

Freedom from Unwholesome Speech

> Let no unwholesome word proceed from your mouth, but only such a word as is good for edification according to the need of the moment, so that

it will give grace to those who hear. (4:29)

"Unwholesome," *sapros* in the Greek, was used to describe rotten fruit.[3] Applied to language, it can refer to several kinds of speech —cursing, vulgar phrases, crude jokes, and unkind or mean-spirited remarks. In our technological society, this includes e-mails too. It's so easy to fire off something that we might never say to a person's face. "Unwholesome," then, refers to anything that is not "good for edification according to the need of the moment." Again, we need to think about the needs of others and focus on imparting "grace to those who hear."

Freedom from Unkindness and Unforgiveness

> Let all bitterness and wrath and anger and clamor and slander be put away from you, along with all malice. Be kind to one another, tender-hearted, forgiving each other, just as God in Christ also has forgiven you. (vv. 31–32)

In verse 31, Paul essentially summed up his other counsel, adding specific traits that flesh out his picture of sin-enslaved living:

- *Bitterness*—a spirit that refuses reconciliation

- *Wrath*—outbursts of anger or a quick temper for selfish reasons

- *Anger*—a nurtured attitude of hatred

- *Clamor*—loud self-assertions of angry people

- *Slander*—destroying others' reputations by lying, gossiping, and spreading rumors

- *Malice*—deliberately trying to harm people[4]

True to Paul's form, he encouraged three godly attitudes of freedom to replace the hurtful ones:

- *Kindness*—acting charitably toward others, just as God has done toward us

---

3. See Stott, *The Message of Ephesians*, p. 188.

4. List adapted from Bruce B. Barton, Philip Comfort, Kent Keller, Linda K. Taylor, and Dave Veerman, *Ephesians*, Life Application Bible Commentary Series (Wheaton, Ill.: Tyndale House Publishers, 1996), p. 97.

- *Tenderheartedness*—being sensitive and sympathetic to others' needs

- A *forgiving spirit*—extending grace and mercy to all who need it

Why be kind, tenderhearted, and forgiving? Because God first acted this way toward us. He even initiated forgiveness before we wanted it!

A Final Thought

In the midst of this passage, Paul added a thought that could have been inserted after any of the five items on his list:

> Do not grieve the Holy Spirit of God, by whom you
> were sealed for the day of redemption. (v. 30)

What does it mean to grieve the Spirit? When we lie, lash out in anger, steal, use hurtful speech, or refuse to forgive, we bring Him pain and distress. We cause Him sorrow. But when we walk in freedom, loving as Christ loved, caring as Christ cared, forgiving as Christ forgave, we delight Him. And we honor the One who saves us from sin's deadly tyranny and secures for us a beautiful future where God's holiness and kindness will reign unopposed.

What a motivation for living free!

✐ *Living Insights*

In his book *He That Is Spiritual*, Lewis Sperry Chafer identified a key activity of truly spiritual people: "They avoid grieving the Holy Spirit by confessing their sins to God."[5]

What sins do you need to confess? Which of the five obstacles to free living mentioned in Ephesians 4:25–32 do you find particularly difficult to release your hold on? Is there someone with whom you need to settle an unresolved conflict?

_____

_____

5. Lewis Sperry Chafer, *He That Is Spiritual* (Findlay, Ohio: Dunham Publishing Co., 1918), chap. 4.

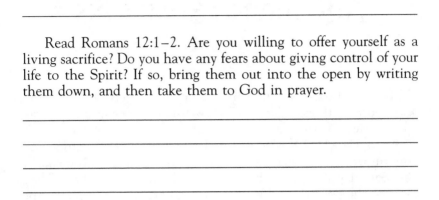

Read Romans 12:1–2. Are you willing to offer yourself as a living sacrifice? Do you have any fears about giving control of your life to the Spirit? If so, bring them out into the open by writing them down, and then take them to God in prayer.

Will you never grieve the Spirit again? We all wish we wouldn't hurt Him with our sins, but, sadly, we know we inevitably will. And so does God: "He Himself knows our frame; He is mindful that we are but dust" (Ps. 103:14). But it means something to Him to know that we don't *want* to hurt Him—that grieving Him grieves us.

So when you sin and wound Him, seek to quickly heal your relationship with Him through honest, heartfelt confession—because He wants your freedom even more than you do!

Chapter 17

A STIRRING SUMMONS TO PURITY

Ephesians 5:1–7

In reading the pages of life, one wise person observed, "A picture is worth a thousand words." How true—especially in the way one life can impact another.

In his book *A Father's Gift: The Legacy of Memories*, author Ken Gire turned to such a snapshot in the photo album of his memory. One Saturday afternoon when he was a child, a "seventeenish" boy came to the door with a briefcase and a practiced sales pitch. His words, though, came out "sideways-sounding," and the young man's face "contorted as he talked." Not knowing quite what to do, Ken got his dad.

His father invited the young, disabled salesman in, and Ken watched him display his wares—thin, sheer "'old men's' socks." Knowing that money never quite stretched to month's end, Ken waited to see how his dad would send this young man on his way.

What his father did surprised him . . . and left an indelible mark on his heart:

> But he didn't send him away.
>> He listened to him with patience,
>> spoke to him with kindness,
>> treated him with respect.
>> He examined the socks,
>> and, to my round-eyed surprise,
>> bought three pairs of those frightful things.
>> Black, brown, and navy, if I remember right.[1]

Ken adds that his dad never told him, "'Son, this is how you treat someone less fortunate than yourself, someone who's disabled or disadvantaged.'" His father just lived out a picture of it for his son. What kind of impact did this have on Ken? His first book was

---

1. Ken Gire, *A Father's Gift: The Legacy of Memories* (Grand Rapids, Mich.: Zondervan Publishing House, 1992), pp. 17, 19. This book was formerly titled *The Gift of Remembrance* (Zondervan, 1990).

about a mentally disabled boy. He volunteers to help people with disabilities. And his heart softens whenever he meets "those who are in some way bent or broken," praying

> that the load they carry
> may be made easier to bear,
> that they may be protected
> from the cruelties of this world,
> and that they may experience as much
> as they can of the goodness
> life has to offer.

And one more thing,
I smile.[2]

In Ephesians 5, Paul wanted us to look at a picture of our heavenly Father and His Son—a picture of the Lord who has reached out and invited us in, treating us with inestimable kindness and dignity. He wanted this picture to imprint its message on our hearts and lives too, so that we would reach out to others with compassion and respect. Let's study the message in this picture and learn to illustrate our Lord's heart in our own lives.

A Living Picture of Love

Truthful and true; just; without sin in anger; caring for others' needs; extending grace, kindness, empathy, forgiveness—all of these qualities in Ephesians 4 reach their summit in chapter 5:

> Therefore be imitators of God, as beloved chil-
> dren; and walk in love, just as Christ also loved you
> and gave Himself up for us, an offering and a sacrifice
> to God as a fragrant aroma. (vv. 1–2)

"Be imitators of God"—this could be a daunting challenge if it weren't for Paul's next phrase, "as beloved children." It's so much easier to grow in an atmosphere where we're loved, isn't it? And it's so natural to become like someone who loves us, just as Ken Gire became like the gentle father he trusted, loved, and admired.

Imitation doesn't come without effort, though. We need to be alert and aware, studying our heavenly Father's ways and seeking

2. Gire, A Father's Gift, p. 23.

to obey His will. As Paul put it, we who are God's cherished children need to follow in His steps—"walk in love"—because these are the steps His Son took. Look at the nature of Jesus' love:

- He "gave Himself up for us": Jesus' life and death were the ultimate act of giving; He surrendered Himself "to the point of death, even death on a cross," in order to rescue us from sin's deadly penalty (Phil. 2:8).

- He also became "an offering and a sacrifice" to God: Through His Crucifixion, Jesus paid the price for our sins, cleansed us from sin, and restored our relationship with God. His willingness to lay down His own life to save us pleased the Father like "a fragrant aroma" (Eph. 5:2).

Jesus' love is self-giving and self-sacrificing—and that's the love He wants us to walk in and live out. As Frederick Buechner explains, "He is telling us to love our neighbors in the sense of being willing to work for their well-being even if it means sacrificing our own well-being to that end."[3]

The world around us, however, opposes Christ's way of love at every turn and tries with all its might to lead us into its doomed pattern (see vv. 5–6). That's why Paul issued such a strong summons to purity—an urgent warning against the world's self-serving ways —in the next five verses.

Strong Words against Love's Enemies

Paul singled out several sins that he didn't want even mentioned in association with the Christian community:

> But immorality or any impurity or greed must not even be named among you, as is proper among saints; and there must be no filthiness and silly talk, or coarse jesting, which are not fitting, but rather giving of thanks. For this you know with certainty, that no immoral or impure person or covetous man, who is an idolater, has an inheritance in the kingdom of Christ and God. (vv. 3–5)

---

3. Frederick Buechner, *Listening to Your Life: Daily Meditations with Frederick Buechner*, comp. George Connor (San Francisco, Calif.: HarperSanFrancisco, 1992), p. 242.

Paul began with sexual sin, not because it's the worst we can do, but possibly because it was so prevalent in that day (and in ours). Remember, Ephesus was the center of worship for the goddess Artemis, also known as Diana, who was the fertility goddess and was worshiped through cult prostitution. In our time (and in theirs), sexual immorality also masquerades as love, pretending to be something far different from the heartbreaking, cheapening counterfeit of God's design for intimacy that it is.

Those reborn in Christ need to know that the deadly corruption of their old ways has no place in their new life—a life of genuine, holy love.

Immorality and Impurity

The Greek word for "immorality," *porneia*, shares a common root with our word *pornography* and includes all kinds of sexual intercourse outside of marriage—including fornication, adultery, and prostitution. "Impurity," *akatharsia* in Greek, speaks of moral uncleanness, and in the sexual sense probably includes homosexuality and any other sexual perversion and excess.[4]

Our Western society actually champions immorality and impurity—nearly any kind of sexual expression is encouraged, as long as both parties are consenting. We don't need to catalog it here; most of us are acquainted with what's on television, in movies, and reported in the newspaper. Many people believe that "free" sex is harmless, that nobody gets hurt.

But Paul warned us not to be deceived with these "empty words" (v. 6), because sin's harm is very real. Sexual immorality only degrades our humanity; it never enhances it. Frederick Buechner observes:

> Our society is filled with people for whom the sexual relationship is one where body meets body but where person fails to meet person; where the immediate need for sexual gratification is satisfied but where the deeper need for companionship and understanding is left untouched. The result is that the relationship leads not to fulfillment but to a half-conscious sense of incompleteness, of inner loneliness, which is so much the sickness of our time. The desire to

4. See James Montgomery Boice, *Ephesians: An Expositional Commentary* (Grand Rapids, Mich.: Baker Books, 1997), p. 180.

know another's nakedness is really the desire to know the other fully as a person. It is the desire to know and to be known, not just sexually but as a total human being. It is the desire for a relationship where each gives not just of his body but of his self, body and spirit both, for the other's gladness.[5]

God has so much more to give us than what we chase after for ourselves. Paul continued in this line of thinking with the next sin he addressed.

Greed

Where immorality and impurity are a lust for sex, greed is a "lust for more."[6] This could include an insatiable appetite for sex, as in a sexual addiction. But it also indicates a hunger for more material possessions.[7] Paul gave greed another name in verse 5, "covetousness," which he directly connected to idolatry—because greed "makes a god of what it seeks to possess."[8]

As author Kathleen Norris observes, "Idolatry makes love impossible" because we have "elevated ourselves and our perceived desires above all else."[9] How can we walk in Christ's self-sacrificial love *and* run after self-centered interests? How can we be consecrated to God *and* dedicated to possessions? How can we give to others *and* grasp all we can for ourselves? We can't. We must choose one or the other, as Jesus told us:

> "No servant can serve two masters; for either he will hate the one and love the other, or else he will be devoted to one and despise the other. You cannot serve God and wealth." (Luke 16:13)

---

5. Buechner, *Listening to Your Life*, p. 264.

6. A. Skevington Wood, "Ephesians," in *The Expositor's Bible Commentary*, gen. ed. Frank E. Gaebelein (Grand Rapids, Mich.: Zondervan Publishing House, Regency Reference Library, 1978), vol. 11, p. 68.

7. See Boice, *Ephesians*, p. 180; and Gerhard Kittel and Gerhard Friedrich, eds., *Theological Dictionary of the New Testament*, translated and abridged in one volume by Geoffrey W. Bromiley (1985; reprint, Grand Rapids, Mich.: William B. Eerdmans Publishing Co., 1992), p. 865.

8. Wood, "Ephesians," p. 68.

9. Kathleen Norris, *Amazing Grace: A Vocabulary of Faith* (New York, N.Y.: Penguin Putnam, Riverhead Books, 1998), p. 88.

Again, God has so much to give us, more than we could ever grasp with greedy hands—eternal riches that infinitely surpass any temporal wealth we could amass here on earth.

Filthiness, Silly Talk, and Coarse Jesting

From immoral actions Paul next turned to immoral words. "Filthiness" means what it sounds like—"shameful talk"—and is linked to the idea of being disgraceful.[10] This would include obscenities, which degrade and abuse others.

The phrase "silly talk" is one word in Greek, *morologia*, and it contains the root (*moros*) that's found in our word *moron*, which denotes a fool. Remember, though, that a fool in Scripture's sense of the word is not a stupid person but one who denies the reality of God. As David wrote, "The fool has said in his heart, 'There is no God'" (Ps. 14:1). Historically, *moros* pointed to "a weakness of understanding or judgment" and "missing [a] true knowledge of God. . . . At root it implies a practical denial of God as the Judge of good and evil" and is "linked with arrogance."[11] Far from good-natured humor, this foolish talk tears down with vulgarity and contempt the things God values.

"Coarse jesting" also comes from a single Greek word, *eutrapalia*, which means "well-turned, versatility, wit." This probably points to forms of humor that depend on a clever turn of phrase, such as double-entendres.[12] Once again, Paul singled out a strength, like a quick wit, that can be used for demeaning, indecent purposes.

Filthy, foolish, and vulgar talk leads us into five danger zones: (1) it plays too near the edge of what can degenerate into grossly inappropriate words and actions, (2) it breaks down our resistance to things that hinder our intimacy with God, (3) it promotes a warped and degrading view of sex and marriage, which God created to be beautiful, (4) it promotes mental habits of sensuality and disrespect for others, and (5) it silences any opportunity to make Christ known. Sensual talk and gutter humor serve no beneficial purpose; even the laughter they provoke turns to bitter dust in our hearts. And worse, they mar the delight God has planned for intimacy with our mates.

10. Kittel and Friedrich, *Theological Dictionary of the New Testament*, p. 30.

11. Kittel and Friedrich, *Theological Dictionary of the New Testament*, p. 620.

12. Wood, "Ephesians," pp. 68–69.

Ramifications of Sin

We know better than to think that sexual self-indulgence, materialistic self-centeredness, and degrading self-expression are "no big deal." Just how big a deal are they? With unflinching directness, Paul warned:

> For this you know with certainty, that no immoral or impure person or covetous man, who is an idolater, has an inheritance in the kingdom of Christ and God.
>
> Let no one deceive you with empty words, for because of these things the wrath of God comes upon the sons of disobedience. (Eph. 5:5–6)

Our behavior shows whose children we are, to whom we belong. When we love like Christ, we reflect that we're members of His family. However, if we habitually choose a lifestyle that opposes God's character and His will, if we blatantly and continually give ourselves to evil so that it becomes our life's pattern, then we need to examine if we really belong to Christ. Constant trafficking in sin is incompatible with the Christian faith.

Does this mean that if, through weakness, we fall into immorality or covetousness, we're not God's children? Not at all. God knows that we're human and that we will sin. The key is whether we deliberately persist in a lifestyle that resists the Lord or whether the general tenor of our lives reflects a Godward direction. Christ, not sin, is to be our way of life.

Advice to Counter Sin

Rather than devoting our gifts to reducing respect for God and His ways, Paul prescribed two righteous courses of action: "giving of thanks" and not being "partakers with" those who practice such sins (vv. 4, 7).

In place of filthy, immoral talk, Paul wanted us to thank the Lord. He was actually recommending that we replace *self-centered* ideas with a *God-centered* frame of mind[13]—that we not abuse God's gifts, such as sexual love and material blessings, but instead praise Him for their beauty and goodness in His design.

---

13. See John R. W. Stott, *The Message of Ephesians: God's New Society,* The Bible Speaks Today Series (Downers Grove, Ill.: InterVarsity Press, 1979), p. 192.

And Paul warned us not to partner with those who live in sin's darkness—not to participate in the ways of "those who have excluded themselves from the kingdom by their impurity."[14] Why would we want to join those whose end is destruction? We have been made "fellow heirs and fellow members of the body, and fellow *partakers* of the promise in Christ Jesus through the gospel" (3:6, emphasis added—this is the same word Paul used in 5:7; see also 2 Cor. 6:14–18). So we need to stay away from those who try to convince us that living close to the edge is acceptable. It's dangerous, and it's contrary to our call in Christ.

If you struggle with some of the sins Paul mentioned, take heart. The Lord knows your grief and shame, and He's reaching out His hand of forgiveness and help. Won't you take it now? He may lead you away from harmful companions. He may lead you to a counselor who can give you intensive help.

Wherever He leads, though, you can rest in the knowledge that it's along the path of love—a path His Son blazed for us and wants to travel with us.

Living Insights

We've spent a lot of time looking at specific sins, but do we fully understand what sin in general does and why God opposes it so fiercely? In his book *Not the Way It's Supposed to Be: A Breviary of Sin*, professor Cornelius Plantinga Jr. shows us how completely incompatible sin is with God's plans for us. His words are well worth your time and meditation:

> The webbing together of God, humans, and all creation in justice, fulfillment, and delight is what the Hebrew prophets call *shalom*. . . . Shalom means *universal flourishing, wholeness, and delight*—a rich state of affairs. . . . Shalom, in other words, is the way things ought to be. . . .
>
> . . . God hates sin not just because it violates his law but, more substantively, because it violates shalom, because it breaks the peace, because it interferes with the way things are supposed to be. . . .

14. Wood, "Ephesians," p. 69.

Sin offends God not only because it bereaves or assaults God directly, as in impiety or blasphemy, but also because it bereaves and assaults what God has made. Sexism and racism, for example, show contempt both for various human persons and also for the mind of God. . . .

In sum, shalom is God's design for creation and redemption; sin is blamable human vandalism of these great realities and therefore an affront to their architect and builder.[15]

Sin not only vandalizes and mars God's design, but, as Plantinga adds, it "distorts our character, a central feature of our very humanity. Sin corrupts powerful human capacities—thought, emotion, speech, and act—so that they become centers of attack on others or of defection or neglect."[16] Think about that; in sin's hands, our God-given capabilities that were designed to do good become "centers of attack on others."

It's frightening, isn't it? And it's unthinkable—or it should be—that anyone redeemed, reconciled, and consecrated to God by the anguished death of His only Son would continue to live in such anti-God ways.

It's Christ's wild, reckless love for us that has rescued us from sin's deadly grip. Let's abandon ourselves to His love and walk according to His design—which is the way things ought to be.

---

15. Cornelius Plantinga Jr., *Not the Way It's Supposed to Be: A Breviary of Sin* (Grand Rapids, Mich.: William B. Eerdmans Publishing Co., 1995), pp. 10, 14, 16.

16. Plantinga, *Not the Way It's Supposed to Be*, p. 2.

Chapter 18

THIS LITTLE LIGHT: IS IT REALLY MINE?

Ephesians 5:6–14

Far off in the dark night, the ship's captain spotted faint lights. Right away, he ordered his signalman to send this message:

> "Alter your course 10 degrees south."
>
> Promptly a return message was received: "Alter your course 10 degrees north."
>
> The captain was angered; his command had been ignored. So he sent a second message: "Alter your course 10 degrees south—I am the captain!"
>
> Soon another message was received: "Alter your course 10 degrees north—I am seaman third class Jones."
>
> Immediately the captain sent a third message, knowing the fear it would evoke: "Alter your course 10 degrees south—I am a battleship!"
>
> Then the reply came: "Alter your course 10 degrees north—I am a lighthouse."[1]

Do you think that captain changed his course? You bet he did! But more than his course changed—his perspective changed as well. The light he first thought was a threat to his vessel was actually its salvation. It warned, "Treacherous rocks ahead!" and pointed him and his crew to safe harbors.

God's light is like that too. We tend to shrink back from it in fear, but with the Spirit's help, we come to see it as our saving grace.

Our passage in Ephesians radiates with the theme of light and its benefits to those who follow it. To help us better understand Paul's metaphor, let's first explore this theme in the context of Scripture as a whole. Our minds and hearts are sure to be enlightened!

---

1. From *Leadership*, Spring 1983, as quoted by Charles R. Swindoll in *The Tale of the Tardy Oxcart*, Swindoll Leadership Library Series (Nashville, Tenn.: Word Publishing, 1998), pp. 539–40.

Light in Scripture

Way back at the dawn of Creation, we see the first rays of God's light creeping over the horizon:

> The earth was formless and void, and darkness was over the surface of the deep, and the Spirit of God was moving over the surface of the waters. Then God said, "Let there be light"; and there was light. God saw that the light was good; and God separated the light from the darkness. (Gen. 1:2–4)

Since the world began, light and darkness have been separated, unable to exist in the same space. As this passage from Genesis shows, one of the purposes of light is to shove back the darkness and bring something good to the formless and void places. Let's consider some of light's other purposes.

The Purposes of Light

First, spiritually speaking, light dispels the darkness of the world so that we can find our way home to God. As Jesus told us:

> "I have come as Light into the world, so that everyone who believes in Me will not remain in darkness. . . . I am the Light of the world; he who follows Me will not walk in the darkness, but will have the Light of life." (John 12:46; 8:12)

When we stumble around in the world's deep shadows, it's as if we've been dropped into the inner chambers of Carlsbad Caverns without a flashlight. We grope around, not knowing whether we'll pitch over a ledge or ever find our way out of the cave's tomb. But with the help of light, our disorientation changes into direction, and our fears melt into hope as we follow its guidance to safety and home.

Second, light attracts attention. Strike a match in a pitch-black room, and people will turn their heads to look. Light invites notice, and spiritual light invites the world's notice. That's why Jesus said, "A city set on a hill cannot be hidden" (Matt. 5:14b). Lives aglow with God's light serve as beacons of hope for far-off travelers seeking rest. And we also serve as searchlights, fanning the skies of our families, neighborhoods, and workplaces to draw attention to the peace and security only the Lord can offer.

The light, however, doesn't originate inside us. It comes from the only Source that can sustain it and always use it for good.

The Source of Light

God, of course, is the source of light. The Bible refers to Him as our "light and . . . salvation" (Ps. 27:1). The prophet Isaiah spoke of Him as an "everlasting light" who will take the place of the sun and moon (Isa. 60:19). In the New Testament, the apostle John said that "God is Light" (1 John 1:5) and that Jesus is the "true Light which, coming into the world, enlightens every man" (John 1:9). In His own words, Jesus declared, "I am the Light of the world" (9:5b).

The light shines through us, but the origin rests in God alone. We are merely lamps, filled with His light and displaying it to the world around us.

Lights in the World

In Ephesians 5:6–14, Paul gave several guidelines to help us keep God's light burning brightly in our lives.

"Do Not Be Partakers"

As we learned in our previous chapter, Paul described a certain category of people who willfully live separated from the light of God: the "immoral or impure person or covetous man, who is an idolater" (v. 5). He warned, "Do not be partakers with them," because "the wrath of God comes upon the sons of disobedience" (vv. 6–7).

The "sons of disobedience" wander all their days in a cavern of sin and its treacherous darkness. Why would we want to follow their blind lead to destruction when we've been called out of darkness and into Christ's light? It doesn't make sense, does it?

Christ leads us up a path to a land luminous with hope and love. He's written us a new passport, in His blood, that allows us to cross over from our old country to the new, heavenly land.

"Walk as Children of Light"

We used to be siblings of the "sons of disobedience"—fellow citizens in a rebel world—but now we have a new Father, a new citizenship, and a new life to live. As Paul put it,

> For you were formerly darkness, but now you are
> Light in the Lord; walk as children of Light. (v. 8)

147

Not only did we live in darkness, but we *were* darkness . . . and now we *are* light. John Stott explains that Paul was playing

> on the rich symbolism of darkness and light, "darkness" representing ignorance, error and evil, "light" representing truth and righteousness. . . . Notice that [Paul] does not say [the Ephesians] used to be *in* darkness, but now were *in* the light. . . . What Paul writes here is more striking still: they themselves were actually now "light." "Their lives and not just their environment" had been changed from darkness to light.[2]

Like the Ephesians, we were also *in* darkness and our lives *were* darkness—we were ignorant and immoral. But now, in Christ, we're in the light, and we have His light illuminating our lives from within.

Since we are light in the Lord, Paul explained that we need to

> walk as children of Light (for the fruit of the Light consists in all goodness and righteousness and truth), trying to learn what is pleasing to the Lord. (vv. 8b–10)

Pleasing the Lord is now our life's goal, and we do this through making morally upright choices and living in integrity.

"Do Not Participate"

In contrast to the good spiritual fruit that grows in God's light are the poisonous and bitter things that fester in the dark. Regarding them, Paul gave us a warning and a strategy:

> Do not participate in the unfruitful deeds of darkness, but instead even expose them; for it is disgraceful even to speak of the things which are done by them in secret. But all things become visible when they are exposed by the light, for everything that becomes visible is light. (vv. 11–13)

---

2. John R. W. Stott, *The Message of Ephesians: God's New Society*, The Bible Speaks Today Series (Downers Grove, Ill.: InterVarsity Press, 1979), p. 199. Used by permission of InterVarsity Press-US and InterVarsity Press-UK. Stott quotes F. F. Bruce, *The Epistle to the Ephesians: A Verse-by-Verse Exposition* (Pickering and Inglis, 1961), p. 145.

Participating in darkness not only hurts fellow Christians but also brings harm to nonbelievers. When we claim to have the light of truth but then lie, defraud others, abuse our children, or live promiscuously—when we don't "walk our talk"—we alienate and confuse non-Christians. Some dismiss us as hypocrites, but others wonder where to find the truth. They may turn away from God completely because of us, vainly seeking light in self-help programs or mystical enlightenment religions. But these paths only lead them into further darkness.

So, rather than participate in the stunted, barren deeds of evil, Paul counseled us to "expose them." Now, let's be very clear about what this means and doesn't mean. Paul didn't intend that we parade other people's sins before a self-appointed moral court. Light doesn't attack; it simply reveals what's there by way of contrast. For example, imagine an office in which all the employees regularly pad their expense accounts and cheat the company. When one worker breaks the pattern and starts behaving honestly, then the dishonesty is exposed. Deeds of light distinguish deeds of darkness, making it possible to evaluate sinful actions against what is right so that others can repent.

Closing Challenge

By refusing to conform to evil behavior, we give off light that penetrates into the deepest darkness of society. Paul understood the great influence believers can have for good, so he issued this challenge, which probably came from a few lines of an early Christian hymn:

> For this reason it says,
> "Awake, sleeper,
> And arise from the dead;
> And Christ will shine on you." (v. 14)

The dawn of redemption has pushed back the covers of night. It's time to wake up and live in the glorious rays of God's Son. Let His light shine!

✣ *Living Insights*

Light is a metaphor for the witness Christians have in the world. Unfortunately, as D. A. Carson laments, Christians have lost their vision for keeping that light in plain view:

> For a variety of reasons, Christians have lost this vision of witness, and are slow to return to it. But in better days and other lands, the faithful and divinely empowered proclamation of the gospel of Jesus Christ . . . so transformed men that they in turn became the light of the world (Matt. 5:14). Prison reform, medical care, trade unions, control of a perverted and perverting liquor trade, abolition of slavery, abolition of child labor, establishment of orphanages, reform of the penal code—in all these areas the followers of Jesus spearheaded the drive for righteousness. The darkness was alleviated.[3]

What a vision! There is real power in the Light.

How well is God's light shining through the lamp of your life? Do you have a vibrant witness where God has placed you? Are you making a difference in your home, in your school system, in your workplace? Or have the pressures and stresses of keeping pace with a busy world dimmed God's light in your life? Has sin crept in and threatened to extinguish whatever flicker of light remains?

_____

_____

_____

_____

Do you feel that how you live your life matters in the greater scheme of things? If not, why?

_____

3. D. A. Carson, *The Sermon on the Mount: An Evangelical Exposition of Matthew 5–7* (Grand Rapids, Mich.: Baker Book House, 1978), pp. 31–32.

The Lord really does want to use you—you play a crucial role in *His* scheme of things! So, if sin has dimmed His light in your life, take time *now* to confess it to Him and ask for His forgiveness and strength to start fresh. Rearrange your schedule so that you spend consistent time with Him in His Word, in prayer, and in your thought life.

And remember the directions Jesus gave us in His Sermon on the Mount, as rendered by Eugene Peterson:

> "You're here to be light, bringing out the God-colors in the world. God is not a secret to be kept. We're going public with this, as public as a city on a hill. If I make you light-bearers, you don't think I'm going to hide you under a bucket, do you? I'm putting you on a light stand. Now that I've put you up there on a hilltop, on a light stand—shine! Keep open house; be generous with your lives. By opening up to others, you'll prompt people to open up with God, this generous Father in heaven."[4] (Matt. 5:14–16 THE MESSAGE)

Hide it under a bushel? No. Let it shine 'til Jesus comes!

4. Eugene H. Peterson, *The Message: The New Testament in Contemporary English* (Colorado Springs, Colo.: NavPress, 1993), p. 16.

Chapter 19

THE CHRISTIAN LIFE 101

Ephesians 5:15–21

P ush!" the nurse in green scrubs urges. "Come on, girl, you can do it! Just one more push and the baby is out!"

"Aaaaaggggggggggghhhhhhhhhhhh!" cries the new mother.

And "Waaaaaaaahhhhhhhhhhh!" cries the newborn baby.

Most of us have either lived through this scene or watched it on television. So we know what the mother does next, right? She breathes a sigh of relief, cradles her miracle in her arms, and coos, "Well, aren't we glad that's over! I'm going home. You take care now and grow up to have a good life. Just call if you need anything, OK?"

I don't think so!

No loving mother says that to her newborn. That baby is fed, changed, bathed, kissed, caressed, rocked, played with, and tenderly watched over. Her cries are comforted; his needs are met. And the parents carefully guide and equip their children for the life ahead of them.

Newborn Christians, though, are often left to fend for themselves. We may labor hard to evangelize them, strain in prayer to bring them to new life in God . . . but then we expect them to grow up on their own.

As you can imagine, this approach doesn't work very well. Young Christians need guidance and equipping for the life Christ has prepared for them. And, to be honest, even "grown-ups" in the faith need to be reminded of some basic truths as well.

That's why Paul called to our minds what it means to be spiritually alive rather than dead, to be centered in truth instead of deceit, to walk in the light instead of in darkness. In Ephesians 5:15–21, he added one more bit of inspired counsel—how to live wisely rather than foolishly.

These truths are as foundational for new believers as they are for the more mature. So let's take Paul's hand as he guides and equips us to grow in our life with Christ.

Growing in Wisdom

Like a father to his children, Paul offered us this piece of counsel:

> Therefore be careful how you walk, not as unwise
> men but as wise. (v. 15)

The word *therefore* connects us with Paul's previous thought—that we are now "Light in the Lord," called to "walk as children of Light . . . trying to learn what is pleasing to the Lord" (vv. 8, 10). Since God has enlightened us and made us His lights in this world, we need to conduct ourselves with care rather than live carelessly—walk wisely instead of foolishly.

Remember, being foolish, or unwise, in Scripture means living as if God doesn't exist (see Ps. 14:1). In contrast, being wise means acknowledging the Lord in all our ways (see Prov. 3:6). Paul addressed four of these ways in the following verses, encouraging us to be mindful of God and distinct from the world in each area.

Time

> Making the most of your time, because the days are
> evil. (Eph. 5:16)

To grow in wisdom means making the most of every opportunity that time provides. The Greek phrase includes the idea of "redeeming time"[1]—or, as Charles Hodge put it, "rescuing it from waste or abuse."[2] Just as Christ redeemed us, rescuing us from a futile existence and giving us new life empowered by His Spirit (see Gal. 3:13–14), so we now have the privilege of using our time for the Lord's purposes. The world ticks to the rhythm of sin, but God wants us to reclaim time for Him.

Since we're still human, however, we're prone to extremes: we tend to either (1) fritter away our time in procrastination, poor choices, and idleness or (2) drive ourselves mercilessly and never relax, rest, and play. Interestingly, both of these extremes leave out God. The first passively resists His purposes for us, and the second disregards the joy of His love.

What can we do to counter these tendencies? We can overcome the first extreme with *discipline*—prioritizing our time and directing our energies into what matters. Discipline involves sacrifice, but

---

1. Bruce B. Barton, Philip Comfort, Kent Keller, Linda K. Taylor, and Dave Veerman, *Ephesians*, Life Application Bible Commentary Series (Wheaton, Ill.: Tyndale House Publishers, 1996), p. 107.

2. Charles Hodge, *Commentary on the Epistle to the Ephesians* (1857; reprint, Grand Rapids, Mich.: William B. Eerdmans Publishing Co., 1994), p. 300.

it's also a form of taking care of ourselves. It helps us accomplish the dreams God gives us and protects the things our hearts value most. Through discipline, we keep sight of how important and useful our lives are to God.

The second extreme can be countered with *discernment*—recognizing that we're not engines but human beings created for relationships with God and family and friends. God has fashioned us to find refreshment in beauty, restoration in sleep, and renewal in laughter. We need to learn that the work of God's kingdom consists of more than just *work*.

Decision-Making

> So then do not be foolish, but understand what the
> will of the Lord is. (Eph. 5:17)

As Walter L. Liefeld observes, Paul's "contrast [between the wise and unwise] continues. The foolish person not only misses opportunities to make wise use of time; he has a more fundamental problem: He does not understand what are God's purposes for mankind and for Christians."[3]

What are God's purposes—His will for His people? Paul explained much about this already:

- to unite everything in heaven and earth under one Head—His Son, Jesus Christ (1:10)

- to accomplish this unity through reconciling people to Himself and to each other by the sacrificial death of His Son (chap. 2)

- to glorify in our lives His grace, which makes reconciliation and unity possible (the whole letter!)

Again, two human extremes often arise regarding God's will: we either run ahead of Him or we resist Him. The first is caused by a lack of patience, and the second results from the presence of pride. Both extremes flare up when we're responding to God's general will for all Christians, which is

> to treat our neighbors as we want to be treated;
> to love the Lord with all our heart, soul, strength, and mind;

---

3. Walter L. Liefeld, note on Ephesians 5:17 in *The NIV Study Bible,* gen. ed. Kenneth L. Barker (Grand Rapids, Mich.: Zondervan Bible Publishers, 1985), p. 1798.

to spread the word about His saving grace;
to feel the joy that comes with sacrifice;
to experience the empowerment that comes
through obedience;
to know the strength that comes by testing.

And these extremes also occur when we react to God's specific will for our lives—choosing a career, a mate, a home, or a church, for example. In fact, we get rather creative in the ways we run ahead of God! Some of us employ the plop-and-point method, letting our Bible fall open and our finger randomly land on the verse to guide the day's choices. Or we decide that a string of green or red traffic signals is a sign. But this "voodoo theology" strays far from how God would have us perceive His will.

Following His lead involves a simple, though not always quick, method. We pray with an open heart. We go to His Word prayerfully and intelligently. We seek the counsel of respected Christians. We wait, listening to His voice in the church's teaching, in its songs, in wise counsel. And when we've discerned His will, we obey it. We may not always perceive it perfectly, but what matters most is walking as best we can in the truth.

Control

> And do not get drunk with wine, for that is dissipation, but be filled with the Spirit, speaking to one another in psalms and hymns and spiritual songs, singing and making melody with your heart to the Lord; always giving thanks for all things in the name of our Lord Jesus Christ to God, even the Father. (5:18–20)

Notice the contrasts Paul set up here: being drunk and out of control versus being under the Spirit's control; having our minds and senses depressed versus having them invigorated and stimulated; squandering time and gifts and life itself versus being made full and complete; becoming dehumanized by alcohol's stupefying effects and robbed of sense and dignity versus becoming more human, as Christ meant us to be.[4]

---

4. See John R. W. Stott, *The Message of Ephesians: God's New Society*, The Bible Speaks Today Series (Downers Grove, Ill.: InterVarsity Press, 1979), p. 205; and Barton and others, *Ephesians*, p. 109.

When people are drunk, the things they say usually profit no one. Their words are either garbled, slurred nonsense or angry vulgarities. When we're controlled by the Spirit, however, our minds are clear to see all that Christ has done and is doing, and we overflow with praise—praise that lifts the hearts of others as well as our own and that honors the Lord. Rather than having a drunkenly bitter and sad heart, the Spirit fills us with joyful gratitude (vv. 19–20)!

If we're wise, then, we won't try to lose ourselves in dead-end escapes, but we'll thirst for the gracious reality of God's presence.

Submission

> And be subject to one another in the fear of Christ.
> (v. 21)

This verse provides a natural setup for Paul's next section, which deals with the relationships between husbands and wives, parents and children, and masters and slaves (5:22–6:9). But it's beneficial to include it here too, because it highlights the integral part humility plays in wise living.

If all of us continually fought to do and have things our way, where would we be? Nowhere. It would be like the wheels of a car pulling in different directions—they'd go flying off, and the car would sit stuck on the pavement.

But for Christ's sake—for the sacrifice He made for us and for the unity of the body He called into being—we need to pull together. And that means giving ground on our own personal desires for the sake of His greater good. Remember what Jesus Himself told us?

> "You know that those who are recognized as rulers of the Gentiles lord it over them; and their great men exercise authority over them. But it is not this way among you, but whoever wishes to become great among you shall be your servant; and whoever wishes to be first among you shall be slave of all. For even the Son of Man did not come to be served, but to serve, and to give His life a ransom for many."
> (Mark 10:42–45)

> "If I then, the Lord and the Teacher, washed your feet, you also ought to wash one another's feet. For I gave you an example that you also should do as I

156

did to you." (John 13:14–15)

And as Paul told us in another of his letters:

> Do nothing from selfishness or empty conceit, but
> with humility of mind regard one another as more
> important than yourselves; do not merely look out
> for your own personal interests, but also for the in-
> terests of others. Have this attitude in yourselves
> which was also in Christ Jesus, who, although He
> existed in the form of God, did not regard equality
> with God a thing to be grasped, but emptied Him-
> self, taking the form of a bond-servant, and being
> made in the likeness of men. Being found in appear-
> ance as a man, He humbled Himself by becoming
> obedient to the point of death, even death on a
> cross. (Phil. 2:3–8)

The wise person, the one who acknowledges God in all his or
her ways, will gently honor and serve others, because in doing so,
Christ is honored.

How Does Your Wisdom Grow?

As you ponder what it means to be "careful how you walk, not
as unwise men but wise" (Eph. 5:15), take a moment to evaluate
the level of your spiritual maturity. Think through the following
questions, and rate how well you're doing on a scale of 1 to 10,
with 1 showing the need for the most growth.

1. Are you careful and wise in your behavior?

    1   2   3   4   5   6   7   8   9   10

2. Are you disciplined and discerning in the way you spend your
   time?

    1   2   3   4   5   6   7   8   9   10

3. Are you actively and correctly pursuing the Father's will?

    1   2   3   4   5   6   7   8   9   10

4. Are you living under the influence and control of the Holy Spirit?

   1   2   3   4   5   6   7   8   9   10

5. Are you deliberately and often finding ways to honor and serve others out of reverence for Christ?

   1   2   3   4   5   6   7   8   9   10

If you aren't doing so well in some areas, there's good news for you. You're not in this alone—you don't have to work at becoming wise all by yourself. As Paul told us, "For it is God who is at work in you, both to will and to work for His good pleasure," and the Lord "who began a good work in you will perfect it until the day of Christ Jesus" (Phil. 2:13; 1:6).

In the Living Insight that follows, take one area in which you need to grow before the Lord, and ask Him to "work for His good pleasure" in your life. The One who has called us to this new life is faithful to help us grow in it (1 Thess. 5:24)—just you wait and see!

✷ *Living Insights*

Which area from our passage do you wish to bring before God? The way you spend your time? The role you let Him play in how you make decisions? What you are allowing to control your life? Your willingness to subject your desires to Christ's greater good?

_____

_____

_____

Why did you choose this area? What's happening to hinder your growth here?

_____

_____

_____

_____

Do you ever find yourself swinging to one of the extremes mentioned in this chapter for this area? If so, which one, and why?

_____

_____

_____

_____

What do you think your life would look like if this area were stronger?

_____

_____

_____

_____

What actions do you need to take to strengthen this facet of wisdom in your life? How do you think God is leading you here?

_____

_____

_____

_____

Remember, God is not your enemy when you are in need. He is your Advocate, and He's eager to help! Jesus even called His Spirit by this name: Helper (John 14:16, 26; 15:26; 16:7). And He encourages us with these words:

> Draw near with confidence to the throne of grace,
> so that [you] may receive mercy and find grace to
> help in time of need. (Heb. 4:16)

Take Him up on it, won't you? Your life will never be better!

Chapter 20

THE MOST CHALLENGING
OF ALL RELATIONSHIPS
(PART ONE)
Ephesians 5:21–24

This next section of Paul's letter pushes buttons. Big buttons. Through ages of misinterpretation and misapplication, Paul's intent to communicate the heights and riches of love in a Christian marriage has often been twisted into a gnarled club to beat women down and "keep them in their place." Tragically, abusive men have commandeered it to justify their cruelty toward their wives, and many in the church have misused it to leave women at the non-existent mercy of violent husbands. Consider this story:

> A woman who rates the abuse she has experienced in her ten years of marriage as severe ("I thought I'd die"), wrote that a Christian counselor she saw said, "'You have to forgive totally and commit yourself 100 per cent'—which I can't—'before God can work on your husband.' . . . He very strongly emphasized that I am to obey my husband despite the violence because I'm really obeying God when I do this, and I need to die to self and see Christ as my all."[1]

That's so wrong! Has not Christ Himself told us, "In everything, therefore, treat people the same way you want them to treat you, for this is the Law and the Prophets" (Matt. 7:12)? And, "A new commandment I give to you, that you love one another, even as I have loved you, that you also love one another" (John 13:34)? In neither of these did Jesus add, ". . . except in marriage."

And Paul didn't add it either. Read afresh what he wrote through Eugene Peterson's rendering:

> Out of respect for Christ, be courteously reverent to one another.

---

1. James and Phyllis Alsdurf, *Battered into Submission: The Tragedy of Wife Abuse in the Christian Home* (Downers Grove, Ill.: InterVarsity Press, 1989), pp. 22–23.

Wives, understand and support your husbands in ways that show your support for Christ. The husband provides leadership to his wife the way Christ does to his church, not by domineering but by cherishing. So just as the church submits to Christ as he exercises such leadership, wives should likewise submit to their husbands.

Husbands, go all out in your love for your wives, exactly as Christ did for the church—a love marked by giving, not getting. Christ's love makes the church whole. His words evoke her beauty. Everything he does and says is designed to bring the best out of her, dressing her in dazzling white silk, radiant with holiness. And that is how husbands ought to love their wives. They're really doing themselves a favor—since they're already "one" in marriage.

No one abuses his own body, does he? No, he feeds and pampers it. That's how Christ treats us, the church, since we are part of his body. And this is why a man leaves father and mother and cherishes his wife. No longer two, they become "one flesh." This is a huge mystery, and I don't pretend to understand it all. What is clearest to me is the way Christ treats the church. And this provides a good picture of how each husband is to treat his wife, loving himself in loving her, and how each wife is to honor her husband.[2] (Eph. 5:21–33 THE MESSAGE)

Paul provided no grounds for abuse here—instead, he gave us a model of loving, mutual submission that works for the other's highest good. As he told us a few verses ago, "Be kind to one another. . . . Walk in love, just as Christ also loved you" (4:32a, 5:2a). Especially in marriage.

The Context of This Passage

Ephesians 5:21 sets out the overarching theme of not only this passage on wives and husbands but also on the following two:

2. Eugene H. Peterson, *The Message: The New Testament in Contemporary English* (Colorado Springs, Colo.: NavPress, 1993), p. 409.

children and parents (6:1–4) and slaves and masters (vv. 5–9). We studied 5:21 in our previous chapter, but let's reread it now:

And be subject to one another in the fear of Christ.

"One another" and "in the fear of Christ" are key thoughts here. Submission isn't a one-way street; rather, it's both people seeking the other's best *and* Christ's honor. Submission gently but firmly displaces selfishness and conceit, competition and pulling rank, domination and dishonor. Specifically, wives treat their husbands with respect, children cooperate with their parents, and slaves (employees) serve their masters (employers) with sincerity and integrity. And husbands, parents, and employers display servant leadership— the same humble leadership Christ modeled for us:

"The Son of Man did not come to be served, but to serve, and to give His life a ransom for many." (Matt. 20:28)

Together we work for Christ's glory, recognizing that we're living testimonies to His grace, life-giving love, and unifying headship over all. Dignity, equality, and unity mark the essentials of submission.

Do you see how important understanding *context* is? It helps us think biblically rather than swing to cultural extremes. And it gives us the ability to reason theologically rather than see things from our narrow human plane.

Now that we have a grasp of Paul's context as a whole, we can safely analyze the separate parts. The first part, which he addressed to wives, is what we'll study in this chapter. Paul's words to husbands will be covered in the next.

A Word to Wives

After urging each of us to be subject to one another, Paul brought this teaching into the home.

Support Your Husband

Wives, be subject to your own husbands, as to the Lord. For the husband is the head of the wife. (Eph. 5:22–23a)

Remember, in Christ we all have dignity, equality, and unity, so Paul's statement here has nothing—*nothing*—to do with inferiority. Men and women are equals, but they do play different and complementary roles. The Lord has designed husbands to provide leadership in the home and wives to support their husbands. He has chosen to order life this way, and we need to trust that He who knows all also knows best.

In our culture, feminists balk at the ideas of roles and submission, possibly because they don't correctly understand God's intent for them. Bruce Barton and his fellow writers give us some valuable clarity:

> This should not be taken to mean that wives are to be doormats, allowing their husband to walk over them; nor are they to be silent partners, wordlessly carrying out their husband's directives. It means that wives are to willingly support their husband's leadership—not balking or undermining him. They are to be active participants in the challenging task of running a Christian home. They are to do everything they can to encourage and support their husbands' leadership in the home, but not blindly or unquestioningly. When the husband is in error or even in outright sin, it is the wife's responsibility to lovingly confront him, pointing him back to the lordship of Christ as the ultimate authority. It takes both partners to make a Christian marriage and home.[3]

Christian marriage means partnership, not tyranny. And God calls women to help their husbands be the best they can be.

Honor the Lord

Notice that Paul added "as to the Lord" in his instruction for wives. Sadly, some men have twisted this to say that a wife should treat her husband as if he were her Lord. Nothing could be further from the truth. We have one Lord—the triune God, made visible in the flesh by Jesus Christ (see John 14:9; 2 Cor. 4:4b, 6; Heb. 1:3). And wives gladly support their husbands *out of their reverence* for the Lord.

Paul explained further:

For the husband is the head of the wife, as Christ

3. Bruce B. Barton, Philip Comfort, Kent Keller, Linda K. Taylor, and Dave Veerman, *Ephesians,* The Life Application Bible Commentary Series (Wheaton, Ill.: Tyndale House Publishers, 1996), p. 113.

also is the head of the church, He Himself being the Savior of the body. But as the church is subject to Christ, so also the wives ought to be to their husbands in everything. (Eph. 5:23–24)

Christ—our Provider, Protector, Head, and Savior—is our supreme role model! If a husband loves and sacrifices himself for the sake of his wife, as Christ did for us, then his wife will joyfully love and sacrifice herself for him in return, as the church does for Jesus.

Now, some of us may have cast a wary glance at the words "in everything." Frankly, some men have co-opted this phrase to justify taking unfair advantage of their wives and abusing the privilege of leadership. But John Stott sets us straight on this account:

> We have to be very careful not to overstate this biblical teaching on authority. It does not mean that the authority of husbands, parents and masters is unlimited, or that wives, children and workers are required to give unconditional obedience. No, the submission required is to God's authority delegated to human beings. If, therefore, they misuse their God-given authority (*e.g.* by commanding what God forbids or forbidding what God commands), then our duty is no longer conscientiously to submit, but conscientiously to refuse to do so. For to submit in such circumstances would be to disobey God. The principle is clear: we must submit right up to the point where obedience to human authority would involve disobedience to God. . . .
>
> . . . Divinely delegated authority . . . must never be used selfishly, but always for those others for whose benefit it has been given.[4]

As Christians, all of us must measure our choices and actions by the same question: Does this honor Christ? As Paul told us in Colossians:

> Whatever you do in word or deed, do all in the name of the Lord Jesus, giving thanks through Him to God the Father. (3:17)

4. John R. W. Stott, *The Message of Ephesians: God's New Society,* The Bible Speaks Today Series (Downers Grove, Ill.: InterVarsity Press, 1979), pp. 218–19. Used by permission of InterVarsity Press-US and InterVarsity Press-UK.

A wife plays a vital role in Christ's order, but she doesn't do it alone. As we'll see in our next chapter, she takes her cues from how her husband leads. And in God's design, the husband follows in Christ's footsteps, making servant-leadership his style.

🖋 *Living Insights*

Perhaps it's not a coincidence that Paul taught about spiritual warfare after giving us instruction on submission (6:10–18). Satan has certainly distorted this teaching, turning God's ideal for our homes and families into his nightmare of abusive torture chambers. Sadly, many people—even people in the church—have believed his lie. What can we do about this? Stand up for the truth. Stand up for Christ's people.

Have you ever been victimized by the distortion of Paul's instruction on submission? Or have you known someone who has? What was the situation, and how was this passage used?

_____

_____

_____

_____

Based on what you've learned in this chapter, how would you define the correct, truly biblical view of submission?

_____

_____

_____

_____

How would you define the biblical view of leadership?

_____

_____

_____

_____

Remember, "'authority' in the biblical usage is not a synonym for 'tyranny.'"[5] If you are being abused or know someone who is, what clarity do the truths of this chapter bring to your thinking? Do you realize that God doesn't sentence women to a lifetime of verbal, emotional, or physical violence? That this isn't His will and design for marriage? Based on what you've learned in this study, describe His design for marriage.

If your spouse is hurting you, or if you know someone who is being abused, don't feel that God wants you or them to take it. He hates violence (see Ps. 11:5), and He longs to protect His children (41:1–2). Pray that God would show you how to get help or give it to someone else.[6] Talk with your doctor, a hospital, a pastor, a counselor, a shelter for abused women, the police, or someone you trust. Above all, get yourself or the person being abused to safety. Don't stay in a place of danger.

And remember, you're not disobeying your husband by confronting and resisting his sin. You are opposing evil. You are opening the way for your husband to face the truth about himself and hopefully come to repentance and get the help he needs. And by doing this, you are honoring Christ.

---

5. Stott, *The Message of Ephesians*, p. 219. Used by permission of InterVarsity Press-US and InterVarsity Press-UK.

6. If you would like to read some Christian books that address the issue of spousal abuse, we recommend James and Phyllis Alsdurf, *Battered into Submission: The Tragedy of Wife Abuse in the Christian Home* (1989; reprint, Eugene, Ore.: Wipf and Stock Publishers, 1998); and the following two books that are available through your library or an out-of-print book service: Grant Martin, *Please Don't Hurt Me* (Wheaton, Ill.: Scripture Press Publications, Victor Books, 1987); and Kay Marshall Strom, *In the Name of Submission: A Painful Look at Wife Battering* (Portland, Ore.: Multnomah Press, 1986). And if your doctor or someone you trust recommends a secular book about escaping battering, get it too. God can bring you help through a variety of means.

Chapter 21

THE MOST CHALLENGING OF ALL RELATIONSHIPS

(PART TWO)

Ephesians 5:25–33

In the balance of his counsel to wives and husbands, Paul went beyond presenting Christ as our model—he intertwined human marriage with Christ's marriage to His church. Like gold, silver, scarlet, and blue threads woven through a tapestry, men and women and Christ and His church are divinely interlaced.

What was Paul's purpose in so closely connecting the two relationships? Dan Allender and Tremper Longman, in their book *Intimate Allies*, show us the deep truth Paul was getting at:

> Marriage is not merely a convenience to overcome loneliness or an expedient arrangement to propagate the race. First and foremost, marriage is a mirror of the divine-human relationship. Every marriage is meant to represent God: his perfect relationship with himself—Father, Son, and Holy Spirit—as well as his relationship with his people. . . .
>
> . . . We can reveal God by the way we love our spouses.[1]

Think of it: marriage, despite the faults of its two very human partners, is meant to reflect Christ's relationship with us. Perhaps that idea should be added to the marriage vows: "To have and to hold from this day forward, for better or for worse, for richer or for poorer, in sickness and in health, to love and to cherish, to reveal Christ to the world and to enhance His presence in each other, till death do us part."

What a beautiful tapestry the weaving together of our lives would be if we kept this as our pattern!

---

1. Dan B. Allender and Tremper Longman III, *Intimate Allies* (Wheaton, Ill.: Tyndale House Publishers, 1995), pp. xviii, xxiii.

Paul's Word to Husbands

As we pick up with Paul's instruction to husbands, let's remind ourselves once more of the overarching theme of this section: "Be subject to one another in the fear of Christ" (Eph. 5:21). For wives, this expresses itself through support and respect. For husbands, it reveals itself in self-sacrificing love:

> Husbands, love your wives, just as Christ also
> loved the church and gave Himself up for her. (v. 25)

Love—it seems so basic, doesn't it? Yet love is crucially important. It's the central thread of Christianity—it reveals God to the world, as Jesus told us: "By this all men will know that you are My disciples, if you have love for one another" (John 13:35). It's our "excellent way" of life (1 Cor. 12:31) that brings meaning and value to all that we do (chap. 13). It's the path God has marked out for us to walk in (Eph. 5:2). And it's the first step of servant-leadership that reveals Christ in marriage.

Notice, Paul centered on *agapē* kind of love, the love that seeks the highest good of the other, even at the price of one's own good—as Jesus Christ did for us.

Love as Christ Loves

Let's learn more about this kind of love from the One who exemplified it best:

> Christ also loved the church and gave Himself up
> for her, so that He might sanctify her, having cleansed
> her by the washing of water with the word, that He
> might present to Himself the church in all her glory,
> having no spot or wrinkle or any such thing; but
> that she would be holy and blameless. (vv. 25b–27)

In this jewel of Christlike love, we find several sparkling facets: sacrifice, help, honor, and desire. Christ surrendered Himself to death on the cross for our eternal good. He cleansed and freed us of sin so that we would be set apart for Him. He perfects and beautifies us with His own radiant glory, readying us to be with Him always when He returns.

How can a husband express this kind of love to his wife? John Stott explains that as Christ's "headship expresses care rather than control, responsibility rather than rule," so should a husband's. He adds:

> The church's head is the church's bridegroom. He does not crush the church. Rather he sacrificed himself to serve her, in order that she might become everything he longs for her to be, namely herself in the fullness of her glory. Just so a husband should never use his headship to crush or stifle his wife, or frustrate her from being herself. His love for her will lead him to an exactly opposite path. He will give himself for her, in order that she may develop her full potential under God and so become more completely herself.[2]

As Christ's love did, so the husband's love will move him to *surrender* his preferences and release having his own way in order to meet his wife's needs. Maybe this means simply turning off the television and listening to what's on your wife's heart. Or maybe it entails something bigger, like staying in one town instead of moving around so much, giving your wife a chance to put down roots so she can grow without fear.

This love will also cause a husband to have a *sanctifying* influence on his wife. He will encourage her growth—intellectually, emotionally, and spiritually. If your wife has a gift for art or a beautiful voice, for example, you can praise her and help her find ways to develop and express her talents. If she has wounds from the past, you can take them seriously and help her get the care she needs, possibly from a counselor. And you can pray, study God's Word, and take part in your church together, as well as help each other conquer sin in your lives. When you love your wife as Christ loves His church, you'll delight in seeking her joy.

Loving like Christ also means *forgiving*. A Christlike husband will embrace grace rather than hold grudges, extend compassion rather than berate with shame, and accept and value his wife for who she is rather than demand the unrealistic standard of perfection. And he will want to *honor* his wife, recognizing her as the precious gift from God that she is. She, too, is made in God's image

2. John R. W. Stott, *The Message of Ephesians: God's New Society*, The Bible Speaks Today Series (Downers Grove, Ill.: InterVarsity Press, 1979), pp. 225, 229. Used by permission of InterVarsity Press-US and InterVarsity Press-UK.

(Gen. 1:26–27) and deserves, as Peter instructed, that you "show her honor as a fellow heir of the grace of life" (1 Pet. 3:7).

Wouldn't we all like to be treated this way? Of course! Jesus recognized this as a strong motive for good when He told us, "Treat others the same way you want them to treat you" (Luke 6:31). And so did Paul, which is why he chose the body as his next illustration.

Love Your Wife as Yourself

> So husbands ought also to love their own wives as their own bodies. He who loves his own wife loves himself; for no one ever hated his own flesh, but nourishes and cherishes it. (Eph. 5:28–29a)

The way a man treats his wife reflects the level of his self-respect. And no man saved and sanctified by Christ has any reason to not respect himself. When the God of the universe values you, you're valuable!

And so is a wife. With the same efforts a husband takes to care for himself, for example, doing what he needs to stay healthy and attractive, he needs to make the same efforts for his wife. A loving husband will *nourish* her—helping her to be fulfilled, to mature, and to grow in the Lord. And he will *cherish* her—tenderly and willingly affirming her through both physical affection and emotional reassurance. The Lord wants a husband's arms to be a safe place for his wife, as the church is in His arms:

> Just as Christ [nourishes and cherishes] the church, because we are members of His body. For this reason a man shall leave his father and mother and shall be joined to his wife, and the two shall become one flesh. This mystery is great; but I am speaking with reference to Christ and the church. (vv. 29b–32)

Christ tenderly cares for us as He does His own body—because we *are* His body (see 1 Cor. 12:27). Through His saving us and making us a new creation in Him (see 2 Cor. 5:17; Eph. 2:15), we are as much one with Him as a husband and wife are "one flesh" with each other through the beauty of sexual union and shared lives. Our bond with Christ cannot be dissolved. And because the marriage relationship represents our union with Christ, God does not want it dissolved either. He created marriage to be a powerful witness to His work of reconciliation and unity—what a high ideal marriage is in God's plan!

In concluding his instructions for and insights into marriage, Paul left us with these words:

> Nevertheless, each individual among you also is to
> love his own wife even as himself, and the wife must
> see to it that she respects her husband. (5:33)

What wife wouldn't support a husband who loved her as much as he loved himself—and as sacrificially, tenderly, and purely as Christ loves His bride? What wife wouldn't respect a husband who followed Christ's gentle model of servant-leadership? All of us long to be loved and respected, nourished and cherished. Let's bring these attitudes and actions into our marriages and watch Christ transform them into a mirror of His awesome grace.

Concluding Thoughts

A good marriage cannot be cultivated in a hurry, so please don't think that you have to master all that Paul has taught in the next week! You can certainly get started on it, but the husband-wife relationship needs to be nurtured over the long haul, as both partners work with equal commitment and effort. Like an intricate tapestry, marriage takes patience and constant checking with the pattern.

When it comes together, though, matching the divine design, marriage takes on sacred depths. It becomes an interlocking of souls so profoundly connected that only the word *mystery* can describe it. Marriage is most certainly worth the effort, and its value is beyond any explanation or price!

Living Insights

"Chains do not hold a marriage together. It is threads, hundreds of tiny threads which sew people together through the years. That is what makes a marriage last—more than passion or even sex!"[3]

How are the threads of your marriage holding up? Are they weaving together a beautiful tapestry that pictures Christ's love? Or

---

3. Simone Signoret, in London's *Daily Mail*, July 4, 1978, as quoted in *The Columbia Dictionary of Quotations*, licensed from Columbia University Press. Copyright © 1993, 1995 by Columbia University Press. All rights reserved. As used on Microsoft Bookshelf 98, © & ℗ 1987–1996 Microsoft Corporation. All rights reserved.

are they fraying a little around the edges? Or even starting to unravel? Take some time to evaluate your marriage and your role in it in light of what you've learned in the past two chapters.

Wives

What is your attitude toward submitting to your husband? Have you been resistant? Have you been afraid that submission meant being a doormat? Do you recognize your husband's leadership? Why or why not?

_____

_____

_____

_____

_____

Do you support and encourage your husband? Do you treat him with respect, even when you disagree with him? How does the idea of serving Christ by helping your husband impact the way you treat him?

_____

_____

_____

_____

_____

How do you seek your husband's highest good? Does this mean catering to his every whim? Or does it sometimes involve loving confrontation? Would he know that you desire the best for him?

_____

_____

_____

_____

_____

Husbands

How are you loving your wife as Christ loves His bride, and how are you not?

_____

_____

_____

_____

_____

How have you viewed a husband's role of leadership in the home? Have you tended more toward tyranny than servant-leadership? Toward being a boss rather than being mutually subject to your wife in the Lord?

_____

_____

_____

_____

_____

How willing are you to surrender yourself for your wife's good? Is her joy and fulfillment a primary concern of yours? How have you helped her see her value to you and your delight in her? How do you encourage and appreciate her gifts? Does your wife feel forgiven and safe in your arms when she has made a mistake or when you have disagreed about something?

_____

_____

_____

_____

_____

Husbands and Wives

What are some ways you can work more for each other's highest good?

_____

_____

_____

_____

In what ways can you both show more love and respect for each other?

_____

_____

_____

_____

What impact does it have on you to know that Christ wants your marriage to reflect His loving union with His church? What changes might this inspire you to make?[4]

_____

_____

_____

Remember, creating a good marriage takes time, patience, effort, and equal commitment from both partners. But when you see the results, you'll not only be happier, you will show the world one of the most beautiful models of God's love they could ever see.

---

4. For some ideas on how to make your marriage better match God's design, read Robert Lewis and William Hendricks, _Rocking the Roles: Building a Win-Win Marriage_ (Colorado Springs, Colo.: NavPress, 1991).

Chapter 22

SECRETS OF A
NURTURING HOME

Ephesians 6:1–4; Proverbs 22:6

F rom the tapestry of marriage, Paul next lingered over the fine
needlework involved in parenting. We're still within his theme
of mutual submission—"Be subject to one another in the fear of
Christ" (Eph. 5:21)—so we'll find Paul instructing both children
and parents. As he'll show us, this relationship is based on respect,
from child to parent and from parent to child.

A Helpful Backdrop

Paul's shift in application to children and parents may unlock
a cedar chest of childhood memories that we may not have opened
for a while. As we approach Paul's instructions on parenting, let's
first take a moment to check our feelings.

Family Memories

Nestled among the baby blankets and toddler's shoes may be
warm feelings of affection from parents who cradled us tenderly and
dabbed our tears. An old baseball mitt or china doll may bring back
recollections of good times spent together or sacrifices made.

But Paul's teaching may also conjure up darker feelings. Images
of a father we vaguely knew or a mother we could never please may
tumble out of our old chest like moth-eaten linens. We long for
nostalgic recollections, but in their place we find only tattered
memories of conflict, anger, and betrayal.

For most of us, the souvenirs of childhood are a blend of happy
and sad—brightly-lit birthday cakes and broken toys, echoes of
giggles and the taste of hot tears. No family is ideal; we all have a
muddled mixture of emotions swirling around our heritage. And we
always will—even if we diligently follow Paul's counsel—because
the words that we'll read (such as *obey, honor, discipline,* and *instruct*)
aren't integers in a math formula. We can't add them up correctly
and . . . *voila!* Perfect family! Real life's not as tidy as that—it's
much messier, but it's also much richer.

Perspective from Proverbs

Though we don't have any formulas, we do have a core method we can organize our parenting efforts around: *nurture.* The wisest man who ever lived told us:

> Train up a child in the way he should go,
> Even when he is old he will not depart from it.
> (Prov. 22:6)

Parents, as Solomon counseled, we need to *hanak,* "train up" or "dedicate," our children from the time they're little to walk in the way *(derek)* of the Lord. Interestingly, the phrase "in the way he should go" can also be rendered "according to his way," meaning the child's way. Commentator Derek Kidner notes that this probably implies "respect for his individuality and vocation."[1] And pastor J. Vernon McGee observes in his down-to-earth way:

> What he is saying is that God has a way He wants him to go, and parents are to find out that way. They are not to bring up a child in the way *they* think he should go, but in the way *God* wants him to go.[2]

Implicit in this is a sensitivity to how God has put our children together, how He has shaped their personalities and bents. We help them discover their gifts and how to use them for God's glory. Conversely, it means that we don't force the Christian faith on them through pharisaical strictness and zeal, which only fosters in them a desire to "stretch their wings and immediately fly south to escape such a wintry exposure to Christianity. . . .

> Anyone resents being run through an impersonal curriculum and revolts against being treated as a nonperson—and children are no exception. At the center of their being, they want to be *known,* intimately and genuinely, and trained in godliness in a personal way tailor-made for them.[3]

1. Derek Kidner, *The Proverbs: An Introduction and Commentary,* Tyndale Old Testament Commentaries Series (Downers Grove, Ill.: InterVarsity Press, 1964), p. 147.

2. J. Vernon McGee, *Proverbs* (Pasadena, Calif.: Thru the Bible Books, 1982), p. 193.

3. From the Bible study guide *You and Your Child,* written by Lee Hough, from the Bible-teaching ministry of Charles R. Swindoll (Anaheim, Calif.: Insight for Living, 1993), p. 2.

Trained in godliness in a personal way tailor-made for them — that's nurturing. That's knowing how your children learn most easily, how sensitive they are, how much encouragement they need, how close they like you to get, and how they need to be disciplined. That's spending lots of time with them — we can't embroider God's ways into the fabric of our children's lives in a hit-or-miss fashion. We need to "teach them diligently" when we "sit in [our] house and when [we] walk by the way and when [we] lie down and when [we] rise up" (Deut. 6:7). Nurturing is a natural, daily part of life. And when we nurture, we determine to set aside our own agendas and accept our children as individuals, patiently helping them develop their gifts and find ways to use them for God's purposes.

With this backdrop of nurture and godliness in mind, let's turn now to Paul's counsel to children and parents.

Paul's Instructions to Children and Parents

Paul drew close to the children first, giving them his instructions as well as reminding them of Moses'.

For Children

> Children, obey your parents in the Lord, for this is right. Honor your father and mother (which is the first commandment with a promise), so that it may be well with you, and that you may live long on the earth. (Eph. 6:1–3)

Obey your parents in the Lord. In essence, Paul was telling children that obedience to their parents is part of how they serve Christ. Jesus Himself, the very Son of God, "continued in subjection" to His earthly parents, Joseph and Mary (Luke 2:51) — even when they didn't understand or encourage His pursuit of God's call on His life (vv. 41–50).

Kids, God has placed your parents in authority over you because you need the wisdom, guidance, and protection they can provide. Your home is a school for life, with your parents ideally teaching and equipping you to live out Christ's gospel and walk in love and righteousness. In God's design, they are *for* you, as a mirror of how God Himself is for you (see Rom. 8:31).

And parents, this command does not give you divine permission to rule over your children as lords and ladies over their subjects. Only one Lord exists, and He wants nurturing parents to have this attitude: "God gave us this child, and we show our submission to *our* Lord by loving and understanding and nurturing His precious gift to us."

Honor your mother and father. Paul then reiterated the fifth commandment God gave Moses in His Law (see Exod. 20:12; Deut. 5:16). Why? To get at an underlying attitude. Children, have you ever obeyed on the outside but on the inside called your mom or dad ugly names? Honoring goes deeper than grudgingly obeying; it means doing what you're told—even if you don't agree—with respect and love.

Now, if your parents want you to do something that would mean disobeying God, then you respectfully obey God instead. But if they love the Lord and are trying to follow His will, then it's right—and even honors Christ—to obey and respect them.

Paul even pointed out that honoring and obeying parents was "the first commandment with a promise" (Eph. 6:2), which was long life in the land of promise for the Israelites (Exod. 20:12). This isn't a guarantee for us but rather a principle for living. Kids, as you honor your parents, you prepare the fertile soil of your soul to one day receive God's authority. And obeying and honoring Him will give you a bountiful harvest of Christlike character traits, such as self-discipline, humility, and integrity, that can give you a stable, happy, and long life.

For Parents

Paul next turned to fathers as heads of families, but the principles apply to both parents:

> Fathers, do not provoke your children to anger,
> but bring them up in the discipline and instruction
> of the Lord. (Eph. 6:4)

The New English Bible begins this verse: "Fathers . . . do not goad your children to resentment." What are some of the goads that fathers (parents) may use to prod their children to resentment? Unreasonable demands that expect more from a child than he or she can meet. Harsh discipline that doesn't match the degree of the offense. Cruel remarks that scratch and bruise a child's self-image. Even what we may think are expressions of love, such as protecting our children or providing for their wishes, may be overindulgence, favoritism, or permissiveness—which embitter a child's heart.

Instead of provoking, which brings children down, Paul said,

"Bring them up." The Greek word, *ektrephō*, also appears in Ephesians 5:29, translated "nourishes":

> For no one ever hated his own flesh, but *nourishes* and cherishes it, just as Christ also does the church. (emphasis added)

As Paul told Christian husbands to follow Christ's example by nourishing their wives, so he now instructed Christian fathers to "nourish" their children. It's the identical goal, but in this case, the two methods are "discipline and instruction." To discipline is to correct the child who is going the wrong way. To instruct is to show the child the right way. And notice, the child's obeying and the parent's nourishing are both done "in the Lord" (6:1, 4). Christ is the center of the relationship. The nearer parents and children draw to Christ, the nearer they draw to each other.

Concluding Principles

What do our children gain from a nurturing home? First, *nurturing parents help their children know who they are.* Our kids need us to show them their strengths. We can encourage our sons or daughters by telling them what we see: "You're good with your hands," or, "You really have a creative flair." Positive words from loving, involved parents deposit precious coins of confidence in a child's storehouse of strengths.

Second, *nurturing parents take time to cultivate their children's individuality.* Attentive gardeners know that each of their plants needs different care—roses need weekly deep-watering, regular fertilizing with rose food, and cutting back in the winter; while azaleas need well-drained soil, acid-type fertilizer, and occasional light pruning throughout the year. Are children any less individual? Of course not! Nurturing parents will take the time to know their children's makeup and work at helping each child's uniqueness blossom and bloom. They'll create an environment where their kids feel safe in being themselves . . . in being who God designed them to be.

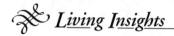 *Living Insights*

For many parents, realizing that although their children are cut from the same genetic cloth but are woven in a unique pattern causes a kind of crisis point. Their different likes, dislikes, aptitudes, and dreams can quickly unravel their parents' long-dreamt-of plans.

Jordan Benedict, the main character in Edna Ferber's epic novel, *Giant*, encountered this crisis moment when he discovered that his three-year-old namesake, Jordie, didn't like riding horses. Disgusted, this father said,

> "I rode before I could walk," he says. "All right," responds his wife Leslie, "that was very cute, but that was you. This is another person. Maybe he doesn't like horses . . ." "He's a Benedict," his father retorts, "and I'm going to make a horseman out of him if I have to *tie* him to do it." "You've been playing God so long you think you run the world." "I run the part of it that's mine." "He's not yours. He's yours and mine. And not even ours. He's himself."[4]

Did your parents allow you to be yourself? Or were they more like Jordan Benedict, wanting to make you into copies of themselves?

_____

_____

_____

_____

How did your parents' perspective toward your uniqueness impact you, positively or negatively?

_____

_____

4. As quoted by John R. W. Stott, *The Message of Ephesians: God's New Society*, The Bible Speaks Today Series (Downers Grove, Ill.: InterVarsity Press, 1979), p. 247. Used by permission of InterVarsity Press-US and InterVarsity Press-UK.

_____

_____

_____

If you are a parent, what challenges do you face in accepting your children as individuals?

_____

_____

_____

_____

Take a moment to read Psalm 139, and reflect on God's creative touch on your children's lives. In what ways can you nurture their uniqueness this week?

_____

_____

_____

_____

The Lord made us in His own image, yet He created us as individuals. In a similar way, our children bear our image, but they are their own persons. Let's enjoy the common threads in our re-lationships with our children while celebrating and nurturing the special pattern God has given them.

Chapter 23

HONORING GOD IN OUR OCCUPATIONS

Ephesians 6:5–9

On Sunday mornings, doesn't the Christian life seem easy? Surrounded by other Christians, listening to sermons and Sunday school lessons, singing inspirational songs . . . it all feels so natural, so right.

But come Monday morning, it's a little harder. That's when we head back to work and we're surrounded with people who live differently from those we're with at church. Maybe they're a little more free in their use of language; perhaps they define *honesty* a little differently than the church does . . . and it's tempting to fall in step with them, to conform to their standards.

This disconnection between our work life and church life is so prevalent that, to many of us, it doesn't even feel wrong. The two don't seem related. Theologian and scholar Dorothy Sayers has commented,

> In nothing has the Church so lost Her hold on reality as in Her failure to understand and respect the secular vocation. She has allowed work and religion to become separate departments. . . .
>
> . . . She has forgotten that the secular vocation is sacred. . . .
>
> . . . How can anyone remain interested in a religion which seems to have no concern with nine-tenths of his life?[1]

We spend most of our waking hours on the job, yet our churches seldom address how Christianity should affect the way we work. The Bible, though, doesn't skip this topic. In our last study, Paul addressed the ways our Christianity should impact our home lives. Today, he'll tell us how to let it permeate our life on the job, reminding us that there is no distinction between "secular" and "sacred" when it comes to the way we act.

---

1. Dorothy Sayers, *Creed or Chaos?* (Manchester, N.H.: Sophia Institute Press, 1999), pp. 106–7.

The Submission of Employees

The wording in Ephesians 6:5 might seem a little strange at first:

> Slaves, be obedient to those who are your masters according to the flesh, with fear and trembling, in the sincerity of your heart, as to Christ.

Could Paul be endorsing slavery here? No. It's important to understand that the issue is not slavery but attitudes. He wasn't addressing the rightness or wrongness of any given situation but the heart of the person in the situation. John MacArthur explains it this way:

> New Testament teaching does not focus on reforming and restructuring human systems, which are never the root cause of human problems. The issue is always the heart—which, when wicked, will corrupt the best of systems and, when righteous, will improve the worst. If men's hearts are not changed, they will find ways to oppress others regardless of whether or not there is actual slavery.[2]

Paul talked to the slaves of that day the same way he would talk to the employees of our day. And what he said, essentially, was that the way we conduct ourselves at work speaks volumes more than all the hours we spend at church. In this verse and the three that follow, he spelled out the kind of behavior a Christian employee ought to exhibit.

Our Response

We see the first element of a godly work ethic in verse 5: *obedience*. Somehow, when we grow up, we tend to think we've escaped the restrictions of our childhood. But the word Paul used here for *obey* is the same one he used in 6:1, when he admonished children to obey their parents. As employees, we have simply exchanged one authority for another. Where we were once responsible to do what our parents required, we are now responsible to do what our bosses require. And we are to do it with "fear and trembling, in the sincerity of [our hearts]" (6:5).

---

2. John MacArthur, *Ephesians*, The MacArthur New Testament Commentary Series (Chicago, Ill.: Moody Press, 1986), p. 324.

What exactly do those words mean? The phrase "fear and trembling" carries the connotation of respect and humility, even honor. The word *sincerity* conveys guilelessness and incorruptibility—in other words, integrity. According to James Montgomery Boice, it also carries "the idea of generosity or liberality. . . . It suggests that the employee should not hold back from his best but should actually pour himself out liberally in honest service."[3] Basically, then, we're to carry out our assignments with honor, humility, and honesty. We're to work hard, pouring ourselves into our jobs, treating our employers with respect.

Sounds good, doesn't it? It's a description we'd all like to see on our performance reviews. But what about those times when your boss seems undeserving of respect? When your assignment seems unnecessary or ill-planned? When, all in all, you think you could do a better job of running the organization?

Notice that Paul didn't include that caveat. He offered no "outs" for difficult situations. But his advice does help us in the area of motivation.

Our Motive

In the secular world, people get respect when they deserve respect. They get cooperation when they deserve cooperation. Paul asked us to honor our bosses whether they deserve it or not. How can we possibly do that?

We can do it because our motivation differs from the rest of the world. Our true aim is not to please our bosses but to please our God:

> Not by the way of eyeservice, as men-pleasers, but as slaves of Christ, doing the will of God from the heart. With good will render service, as to the Lord, and not to men. (vv. 6–7)

Boice calls this perspective the key to the entire passage. Giving respect to an employer, he says, "is made easier by the thought that the employee ultimately serves Christ, even in a difficult situation."[4]

---

3. James Montgomery Boice, *Ephesians: An Expositional Commentary* (Grand Rapids, Mich.: Baker Books, 1997), p. 220. Used by permission.

4. Boice, *Ephesians*, p. 220. Used by permission.

And focusing on our heavenly reward encourages us too:

> Knowing that whatever good thing each one does,
> this he will receive back from the Lord, whether
> slave or free. (v. 8)

As employees, we receive a paycheck for the work we do, unlike the slaves of Paul's time. But that reward is temporary and soon spent. The reward God offers us is eternal. Your employer may not appreciate everything you do—he or she may not even *see* everything you do. But God sees, and He won't forget your diligent, wholehearted efforts (see Heb. 6:10).

The Submission of Employers

Next Paul addressed masters, or employers:

> And masters, do the same things to them, and
> give up threatening, knowing that both their Master
> and yours is in heaven, and there is no partiality
> with Him. (Eph. 6:9)

That one verse covers a broad scope. In essence, Paul applied his words for employees to employers as well. They, too, are to please the Lord in their work, particularly in their treatment of those under them. But Paul's instructions went a step further. He not only told them what they were to do, he also told them something there were *not* to do: threaten their employees.

An old expression fits here: You draw more flies with honey than you do with vinegar. Proverbs also offers some fitting wisdom:

> The generous man will be prosperous,
> And he who waters will himself be watered. (11:25)

> A man will be satisfied with good by the fruit of his
> words,
> And the deeds of a man's hands will return to him.
> (12:14)

> There is one who speaks rashly like the thrusts of a
> sword,
> But the tongue of the wise brings healing. (12:18)

It makes good, practical sense to treat your employees with kindness—after all, the attitudes you model to them are likely to be the ones you get back. But whether your employees deserve it or not, it's what the Lord requires of you. Employers, like parents, stand in a position of power. And like parents, their power should not be used to control but to guide.

Why is it so important to treat employees with respect? Because with God "there is no partiality." Employers and employees are equals in God's eyes, and both will someday stand before the Lord and account for their attitudes and actions.

Eugene Peterson sums up Paul's message in our own words:

> Servants, respectfully obey your earthly masters but always with an eye to obeying the *real* master, Christ. Don't just do what you have to do to get by, but work heartily, as Christ's servants doing what God wants you to do. And work with a smile on your face, always keeping in mind that no matter who happens to be giving the orders, you're really serving God. Good work will get you good pay from the Master, regardless of whether you are slave or free.
>
> Masters, it's the same with you. No abuse, please, and no threats. You and your servants are both under the same Master in heaven. He makes no distinction between you and them.[5] (Eph. 6:5–9 THE MESSAGE)

The world doesn't watch us at Sunday school or in Bible studies but in our work. So let's "work heartily, as for the Lord" (Col. 3:23), then, so that Christ's saving grace and love may be clearly seen.

✣ Living Insights

For the Christian, there's no such thing as "sacred" or "secular." It's all sacred! Whether you're an ordained minister or a plumber or a teacher, you are working for the Lord.

Paul urged us to do our jobs "with fear and trembling, in the sincerity of [our hearts], as to Christ." Listed below are some characteristics of people who approach their jobs in that way. Add some

---

5. Eugene H. Peterson, *The Message: The New Testament in Contemporary English* (Colorado Springs, Colo.: NavPress, 1993), pp. 409–10.

more of your own, and then rank yourself on a scale of one to ten, according to how well you do in that area.

Timeliness

1   2   3   4   5   6   7   8   9   10

Respectfulness

1   2   3   4   5   6   7   8   9   10

Integrity

1   2   3   4   5   6   7   8   9   10

_____

1   2   3   4   5   6   7   8   9   10

_____

1   2   3   4   5   6   7   8   9   10

_____

1   2   3   4   5   6   7   8   9   10

Do you approach your job differently if you regard God as your true employer? If so, what things might you begin to do differently?

_____

_____

_____

God's standards for employment are few: that we perform our work with diligence and that we treat others with respect and care. Those aren't too bad, are they? Especially when viewed in light of God's priorities—the saving of souls for eternal life.

Chapter 24

STANDING FIRM AGAINST SATANIC SCHEMES

Ephesians 6:10–13

A mighty fortress is our God,
A bulwark never failing;
Our helper He amid the flood
Of mortal ills prevailing.
For still our ancient foe
Doth seek to work us woe—
His craft and power are great,
And, armed with cruel hate,
On earth is not His equal.[1]

Martin Luther may have penned the words to this great hymn, but Paul's words in Ephesians 6:10–13, our passage for today, were likely his inspiration. Though we don't hear bombs bursting in the distance or bullets zinging past us, though we don't see the bayonets flashing before our faces, we live every day of our lives on a battleground. Satan has us in the crosshairs of his scope. He studies us intently. He knows our backgrounds, he's familiar with our vulnerabilities, and he's well acquainted with our weaknesses and our strengths. And he uses his knowledge to great advantage, stalking our every step, laying snares in our path.

Whether you're young or old, athletic or academic, a new believer or a seasoned Christian, Satan has one goal for you—your downfall. He hopes not just to cripple you but to ruin you. His own ultimate doom is certain, but he intends to bring you down on his way.

Paul, though, wanted to keep us standing. Even in the hail of artillery fire that continually rains down upon us, he said, we can be safe from Satan's schemes. But we can't do it on our own.

Parts of this chapter are adapted from "Needed: A Godly Mind," from the Bible study guide *Solomon*, rev. ed., written by Ken Gire, from the Bible-teaching ministry of Charles R. Swindoll (Anaheim, Calif.: Insight for Living, 1994).

1. Martin Luther, "A Mighty Fortress Is Our God," trans. Frederick H. Hedge, in *Hymns for the Family of God* (Nashville, Tenn.: Paragon Associates, Inc., 1976), no. 118.

Our Strength Is in the Lord

Paul's battle cry rings out in verse 10:

> Finally, be strong in the Lord and in the strength of
> His might.

Paul's urging us to "be strong" implies that a source of strength will be made available to us,[2] and it is—in our Lord. Only through the Lord's strength will we be able to stand and fight in this ongoing spiritual battle.

Satan would like nothing better than for us to picture him as the little imp on our shoulder, whispering naughty ideas into our ears. As long as we think of him as a pesky little fellow we can brush away like a mosquito, we won't notice just how insidious he really is. But Paul, warming up to the theme he was about to address, warned us that we're no match for Satan and his demons. Only when we rely on Christ's strength can we hope to defeat such a devious and powerful foe.

Remember Paul's prayer at the beginning of this letter? He asked that believers might know "the surpassing greatness of His power" and "the strength of His might" (1:19). And now we see why. Our enemy is strong, and his attacks are relentless. No matter how much we know about the way God wants us to live, no matter how much we long to please Him, we will fall flat on our faces without His help . . . because Satan lies in wait to trip us up at every turn. But we have this hope: The same power that raised Christ from the dead is available to us today.

Our Protection Is in the Lord's Armor

Continuing his call to arms, Paul instructed the Ephesians on how to employ God's strength:

> Put on the full armor of God, so that you will be
> able to stand firm against the schemes of the devil.
> . . . Therefore, take up the full armor of God, so
> that you will be able to resist in the evil day, and
> having done everything, to stand firm. (6:11, 13)

2. See Bruce B. Barton, Philip Comfort, Kent Keller, Linda K. Taylor, and Dave Veerman, *Ephesians*, The Life Application Bible Commentary Series (Wheaton, Ill.: Tyndale House Publishers, 1996), p. 127.

We fight a spiritual battle, and only spiritual armor can protect us. If the enemy were bacteria, our defense might include penicillin. If the enemy were an army, our defense might include guns, tanks, and planes. But when the enemy is the Devil, our only defense is the armor of God.[3]

Notice what God's armor enables us to do: "stand firm" (see also v. 14). We have a fearsome enemy, but when we're protected by God's armor, we have no reason to be afraid. We don't need to cower or run in terror. In Christ, our victory is certain; the battle's outcome has already been determined. It is true that our "adversary, the devil, prowls around like a roaring lion, seeking someone to devour" (1 Pet. 5:8), but when we resist him with the armor of God, he flees our presence like a frightened mouse (James 4:7).

Our Strategy Is Based on Satan's Methods

Next, Paul unrolled the map of spiritual warfare that reveals the Enemy's hiding places:

> For our struggle is not against flesh and blood, but against the rulers, against the powers, against the world forces of this darkness, against the spiritual forces of wickedness in the heavenly places (Eph. 6:12)

We can't see, touch, or feel Satan. He fights us in ways that are hard to detect, and he utilizes an organized hierarchy of demonic rulers, powers, and forces of darkness and wickedness to fight his battles. Remember what verse 11 said? We put on God's armor so that we can "stand firm against the schemes of the devil." Since his schemes are not always visible to us, we need to take a good look at his methods of attack in order to fight back with power.

Satan's Schemes

The word *schemes* in 6:11 comes from the Greek word *methodeia*. The word is plural, letting us know that Satan has more than one method for undermining us. Second Corinthians 2:10–11 gives us an example of one method—an attitude of unforgiveness:

> But one whom you forgive anything, I forgive also; for indeed what I have forgiven, if I have forgiven

---

3. We'll discuss the specific elements of the armor of God in chapter 25.

anything, I did it for your sakes in the presence of
Christ, so that no advantage would be taken of us
by Satan, for we are not ignorant of his schemes.

The word *advantage*, *pleonekteō* in the Greek, means "to take
advantage of, to gain, to overreach."[4] When we harbor anger or fail
to forgive others, for instance, we give Satan an advantage . . .
an open door . . . an entrance (see also Eph. 4:26–27). Our un-
willingness to forgive lays out a welcome mat for him to get the
better of us.

Paul added an interesting insight to Satan's ploys by changing
the Greek word for *schemes* in 2 Corinthians 2:11. He used *noema*,
which means "thought, purpose." It has at its root the term *nous*,
meaning "mind."[5] Paul didn't want us to be ignorant of the fact
that Satan has his sights set on us, especially our minds. Satan will
take advantage of us by using whatever mind schemes he has at
hand, be it unresolved personal conflicts or consuming bitterness,
to draw us away from God.

How does he try to gain control of your thoughts or actions?
Maybe he makes you feel worthless or hopeless. Perhaps he lures
you with temptations. It's worth taking note of his favorite schemes
so you can ready yourself for his assaults.

Our Strategy

How can we prepare for Satan's attacks on our minds? For one
thing, we have to assemble the right weapons:

For though we walk in the flesh, we do not war
according to the flesh, for the weapons of our warfare
are not of the flesh, but divinely powerful for the
destruction of fortresses. (10:3–4)

To fight against spiritual enemies, we need spiritual weapons.
And one of the most "divinely powerful" weapons is the Word of
God. Most of our weapons are defensive, but the Word of God is
one of our few offensive weapons, listed at the end of Paul's itemized

---

4. Archibald Thomas Robertson, *Word Pictures in the New Testament* (Grand Rapids, Mich.:
Baker Book House, 1931), vol. 4, p. 217.

5. Gerhard Kittel and Gerhard Friedrich, eds., *Theological Dictionary of the New Testament*,
translated and abridged in one volume by Geoffrey W. Bromiley (1985; reprint, Grand Rapids,
Mich.: William B. Eerdmans Publishing Co., 1992), p. 637.

arsenal in Ephesians 6—"the sword of the Spirit, which is the word of God" (v. 17). We can wield the Word of God like the sword of Excalibur in the Arthurian legends to cut and penetrate our spiritual foe like no earthly weapon can. Just as Jesus countered Satan's temptations in the wilderness by quoting Scripture, we can thrust God's Word in the Devil's face when we feel attacked (see Matt. 4:1–11). The truth of Scripture exposes his lies and renders his schemes powerless.

Paul said that our spiritual weapons are so powerful they can destroy "fortresses" (2 Cor. 10:4). This word picture is drawn from ancient biblical history, when strategic cities were surrounded by fortified walls of defense. Within these walls were carefully placed towers, built higher than the highest point of the surrounding wall. They served as observation posts for the battle strategists, who were flanked by buglers sounding signals of charge or retreat to the soldiers. For a city to be conquered, the walls had to be scaled, the towers seized, and the strategists captured.

In our battle against the Enemy, we need to destroy such fortresses—high towers that Satan occupies and vigilantly defends with his minions. In the next verse, however, Paul showed us that the power of God's Word can break through and claim this territory for Christ:

> We are destroying speculations and every lofty thing raised up against the knowledge of God, and we are taking every thought captive to the obedience of Christ. (v. 5)

The Greek word for *speculations*, *logismos*, means "the prejudiced thoughts that occupy your mind . . . the designs of the heathen."[6] It refers to the prejudiced thoughts Satan places in our minds that distort the truth, the heathen's designs that appeal to our flesh and cause us to ignore what is right and true.

God's Word allows no place for these kinds of human speculations. He authored right and wrong, truth and fiction, life and death, so He determinedly uses His living and powerful Word to destroy the speculations that would imprison us and to tear down "every lofty thing" that would ensnare us.

---

6. Walter Bauer, A *Greek-English Lexicon of the New Testament and Other Early Christian Literature*, 2d ed., revised and augmented by F. Wilbur Gingrich and Frederick W. Danker, from Walter Bauer's 5th ed., 1958 (Chicago, Ill.: University of Chicago Press, 1979), p. 477.

These "lofty things" work hand in hand with speculations, but they seek to remove the guilt of wrongdoing. They whisper, "That's okay, everybody does that. . . . It's not your fault, your parents made you that way. . . . Compared to other people, you're an angel!" Utilizing excuses, blame-placing, and comparisons, the lofty things work hard to free us from the truth. But, in reality, the most freeing thing we can do is bring our lives captive to the Truth, Jesus Christ (see John 14:6). And since Satan deals in lies and deception, his strategies crumble when confronted with truth.

Four Principles to Stand On

Now that we have Satan's strategy mapped out and have armed ourselves with the spiritual weapon of God's Word, let's build our confidence for battle by standing on four principles.

No satanic assault is stronger than God. Satan's forces are strong, there's no doubt about that. And he can easily defeat us if we try to fight him in our own strength. But we don't have to fear—God is stronger, and we'll prevail if we trust in Him and rely on His strength.

No satanic scheme can penetrate God's armor. We'll learn more about the armor we wear in the next chapter. If we put it on and keep it on, Satan can't injure us.

No satanic force can defeat God's work. God is sovereign, and the conclusion of His plan is already established—He will win the battle.

No satanic evil can prevail over the prayers of God's people. Prayer is essential to victory in the spiritual war. Without it, our communication with our Leader is cut off, and we're bound to get trapped behind enemy lines. Prayer allows us to inform God of our needs and to get direction from Him about where to go and how to fight.

In the next chapter, we're going to look at the armor of God, which we need to put on every day before walking into battle. For now, though, let's just make sure that our minds are ready, that we know how to stand firm against Satan's schemes. And keep in mind the second verse of Luther's gripping hymn:

> Did we in our own strength confide,
> Our striving would be losing,
> Were not the right man on our side,
> The man of God's own choosing.
> Dost ask who that may be?
> Christ Jesus, it is He—

Lord Sabaoth His name,
From age to age the same,
And He must win the battle.[7]

❧ *Living Insights*

Satan is a cunning strategist.[8] In what many consider to be
C. S. Lewis' most famous work, *The Screwtape Letters*, the author
created a correspondence between an elderly devil, Screwtape, and
his young nephew, Wormwood. Screwtape's fictitious counsel to the
eager Wormwood reveals something of the true schemes of Satan:

> You will say that these are very small sins; and
> doubtless, like all young tempters, you are anxious
> to be able to report spectacular wickedness. But do
> remember, the only thing that matters is the extent
> to which you separate the man from the Enemy. It
> does not matter how small the sins are, provided
> that their cumulative effect is to edge the man away
> from the Light and out into the Nothing. Murder is
> no better than cards if cards can do the trick. Indeed,
> the safest road to hell is the gradual one—the gentle
> slope, soft underfoot, without sudden turnings, with-
> out milestones, without signposts.[9]

Is there something in your life that is distancing you from
God—inching you away from the Light? It may be something small.
It may be something good—even religious. Take some time now
to bring it out of its dark hiding place by writing it down.

_____

_____

_____

7. Luther, "A Mighty Fortress Is Our God," no. 118.

8. This Living Insights is adapted from "It Starts in Your Mind," from the Bible study guide
Living above the Level of Mediocrity, rev. and exp., written by Ken Gire, from the Bible-
teaching ministry of Charles R. Swindoll (Anaheim, Calif.: Insight for Living, 1994).

9. C. S. Lewis, *The Screwtape Letters*, bound with *Screwtape Proposes a Toast*, rev. ed. (New
York, N.Y.: Macmillan Publishing Co., 1982), p. 56.

_____

_____

How does this subtle something take you away from God? What is it softly whispering in your ear?

_____

_____

_____

_____

_____

In the days to come, train yourself to listen for Satan's scheming. He may use a tactic that's barely detectable. But if it's a wedge, it will distance you from the Lord.

Chapter 25

STRONG ARMOR FOR WEAK SHEEP

Ephesians 6:13–20

When Paul wrote his letter to the Ephesians, he lingered under house arrest, waiting to appear before Caesar. We can read about his two-year wait in the last few verses of Acts, but in the last chapter of Ephesians, we can also see that though his body was imprisoned, his mind remained free and active.

Guarded by Caesar's brightest and best day after day, Paul closely observed the soldiers' armor. Studying the helmet, breastplate, belt, boots, shield, and sword, he began to think about battles. In a physical battle, the soldiers would be well protected. But in a spiritual battle, all their equipment would be useless. They'd be as helpless as sheep being led to slaughter.

Yet "sheep" is how God often refers to His own people. Sheep who wander off (Isa. 53:6). Sheep who get lost (Luke 15:4–7). Sheep who are helpless (Matt. 9:36). Sheep who need constant, faithful care (Ezek. 34). Faced with a lion or a wolf, sheep are likely to shiver together in a woolly cluster and be eaten one by one. They don't have any claws, fangs, quills, speed, or even a skunk's noxious odor with which to protect themselves.

Like sheep, we Christians can't defend ourselves against the lion who prowls after us (1 Pet. 5:8)—at least not in our own strength. Thankfully, our Shepherd has armed His sheep with spiritual armor that can rout our demonic enemies. Through the Lord's provision and alliance, we can be sheep who "overwhelmingly conquer" (Rom. 8:37).

The Christian's Armor

In Ephesians 6:10–12, Paul described the spiritual battle that rages around Christians every day. He gave us a picture of our Enemy, and then he encouraged us to stand against him in God's power:

> Therefore, take up the full armor of God, so that you will be able to resist in the evil day, and having done everything, to stand firm. (v. 13)

196

We may be weak as sheep, and we may have to rely on our Shepherd's strength, but we are not without a role in this battle. Notice the verbs in this verse: *take up, resist, stand.* If we're going to win this fight, we'll need to actively participate. And we'll need to stand firm in the protection God has provided. Let's try on each piece Paul presented and learn to wield it with precision and mastery.

The Belt of Truth

> Stand firm therefore, having girded your loins with truth. (v. 14a)

Most of us don't "gird our loins" these days; we would buckle a belt around our waist (compare the NIV's wording). The belt on a Roman soldier's uniform, however, did more than make his toga fashionable. Made of leather and about six inches wide, it secured his tunic so that the material wouldn't hamper his movements. It also helped hold in place the breastplate and the sheath for the sword.[1] The belt kept him free, protected, and ready to defend himself.

Our protective belt is made of truth—the truth of God, which is revealed in the Bible, as well as truth of character, or integrity.[2] In the heat of battle, when flaming words of anger are flying above and beside us and unjust accusations are bursting all around, it's tempting to retreat into a lie to save our skin. It can seem so much safer to let what is false have the final say. But Jesus wants us to hold fast to what's true, because He is truth (see John 14:6). That's why Paul urged us to keep that belt pulled tight, to not loosen our integrity. As Christ's representatives, we're to stay true to what the Bible says is right, because that's really what will make us most safe.

The Breastplate of Righteousness

> Put on the breastplate of righteousness. (Eph. 6:14b)

The Roman breastplate was a large piece of leather, bronze, or chain-mail that covered both the back and front of a soldier from his neck to his thighs. It protected the vital organs and was an essential piece of armor, one no soldier would go into battle without.

---

1. See Bruce B. Barton, Philip Comfort, Kent Keller, Linda K. Taylor, and Dave Veerman, *Ephesians*, Life Application Bible Commentary Series (Wheaton, Ill.: Tyndale House Publishers, 1996), p. 131.

2. See James Montgomery Boice, *Ephesians: An Expositional Commentary* (Grand Rapids, Mich.: Baker Books, 1997), p. 244.

Righteousness is our breastplate because it assures us that we have been made right with God through the blood of Jesus Christ and are saved—forever. Theologians describe this as *positional* or *imputed* righteousness. In addition, this breastplate, like truth's belt, is also the righteous lives we live with the Spirit's help.

The breastplate of righteousness is as essential to us as the Roman soldier's breastplate was to him. Our Enemy (whom John called "the accuser" in Revelation 12:10) loves to sling his arrows at the heart of our faith, trying to convince us that God can't bridge the gap our sins have created and to pull us back into sin's hopeless grip. But when we stand firm in the knowledge that Christ has declared us righteous and empowers us to live holy lives, the Enemy retreats in defeat.

The Boots of Peace

> Having shod your feet with the preparation of the gospel of peace. (Eph. 6:15)

Paul had spent many long hours looking at the boots of his jailer. Called the *caliga*,[3] it was an open-toed leather boot with a nail-studded sole, and it was tied to the ankles and shins with leather straps. Obviously, these *caligas* were not used for fleeing or pursuing enemies. Rather, they were used in hand-to-hand combat. Like today's football and soccer cleats, they were meant to give maximum footing and traction to prevent sliding, thus giving the Romans the edge in the trenches of war.

Our "footing" against Satan is our peace with God. Christ has secured this peace (Eph. 2)—peace not only with God but also with each other and within ourselves. As a result of this peace, our Lord will never condemn us (Rom. 8:1). Satan may push all he wants, trying to convince us that God will reject and judge us when we mess up. But if we know that we have peace with God—if we're wearing our boots—then we won't slip and fall. We'll stand stable and firm against the devil's arguments. And we'll gain ground against his opposition so that we can spread the Good News of peace with God through Christ to the troubled world around us.

---

3. See R. Kent Hughes, *Ephesians: The Mystery of the Body of Christ*, Preaching the Word Series (Wheaton, Ill.: Crossway Books, 1990), p. 232.

The Shield of Faith

> In addition to all, taking up the shield of faith with which you will be able to extinguish all the flaming arrows of the evil one. (Eph. 6:16)

The shield Paul had in mind was the Roman *scutum*, a four-and-a-half-foot oval of hide-covered wood, framed with iron.[4] The leather was soaked in water prior to battle in order to put out the enemy's dangerous incendiary missiles—arrows dipped in pitch and lit with fire. "In battle this [shield] could be locked together with others to form a wall in front, and a roof overhead."[5]

The "flaming arrows of the evil one" can take many forms: temptation, doubt, anger, pride, despair, fear, guilt, shame, confusion. They also include persecution and occultic assaults—and anything that would attempt to tear apart the unity of Christ's body. How would faith shield us from such insidious weapons? Max Turner explains:

> Faith in this letter is the radical openness to God that allows Christ's full indwelling, and brings a deeper grasp of his unfathomable love (*cf.* 3:17). *Take up the shield of faith* thus suggests a deliberate and positive holding on to the God revealed in the gospel; firm and resolute dependence on the Lord which quenches the fiery attempts of the enemy to harm and to spread panic.[6]

Through faith, we see our circumstances through God's eyes, trust in Him to keep us from temptation and doubt, and stand safely behind the shield of His protection (see Prov. 30:5).

The Helmet of Salvation

> And take the helmet of salvation. (Eph. 6:17a)

The Roman soldiers' helmets were made of leather and brass,

---

4. See John R. W. Stott, *The Message of Ephesians: God's New Society*, The Bible Speaks Today Series (Downers Grove, Ill.: InterVarsity Press, 1979), p. 281.

5. Max Turner, "Ephesians," in *New Bible Commentary: 21st Century Edition*, 4th ed., rev., gen. ed. D. A. Carson, R. T. France, J. A. Motyer, and G. J. Wenham (Downers Grove, Ill.: InterVarsity Press, 1994), p. 1244.

6. Turner, "Ephesians," p. 1244.

or sometimes bronze and iron. They featured a band to protect the forehead and plates for the cheeks, and they left little of the head exposed to danger.

The Christian's helmet is salvation. Satan would like nothing better than to aim his arrows into our minds, convincing us that we do not belong to Christ. He would like to rob us of the hope of our eternal future in heaven, of our confidence in Christ's ultimate and complete victory over all the forces of evil. Without the assurance of our salvation—or that there is even anything to be saved from—the battle would not be worth fighting. But when we're assured that Jesus is Victor and nothing can snatch us out of His hands (John 10:28), then our minds are safely protected against Satan's attacks.

The Sword of the Spirit

Have you noticed that all our equipment for spiritual warfare so far has been defensive? We're not supposed to retaliate, to return fiery arrows of our own, to take revenge (see Rom. 12:17–21). Instead, we have only one offensive weapon—God's word of truth:

> And [take] the sword of the Spirit, which is the word of God. (Eph. 6:17b)

The sword Paul referred to here was the Roman short sword used in hand-to-hand combat. Razor-sharp and very light, it was a highly effective weapon in the Roman army's arsenal.

The Christian's sword is Scripture and its principles, which are inspired by the Holy Spirit (see 2 Tim. 3:16). This is why it's so important to study God's Word and memorize it—the Lord's words have the power of life in them! Remember what the writer to the Hebrews told us?

> For the word of God is living and active and sharper than any two-edged sword, and piercing as far as the division of soul and spirit, of both joints and marrow, and able to judge the thoughts and intentions of the heart. (Heb. 4:12)

God's words are alive and powerful; they "[override] obstacles and human opinions . . . grasping and sanctifying believers. As the word of grace, life, or salvation, [God's Word] does not just preach these things but effects them."[7] So, with God's Word in our hearts and hands, we have the power to effect change—to counter Satan's destructive forces. Illuminating this power and warning us about how to wield it, Max Turner notes that we are

> to strike back with truth when we are personally tempted to evil; to strike back with truth when the church is attacked by false teaching; to strike back with truth when the powers seek to pervade the world around us with alien philosophies and ethical teaching; and finally to strike vigorous blows for freedom with the fearless proclamation of Christian truth. . . . We are fighting the spiritual powers not human enemies (12). Our use of *the sword of the Spirit* has to reflect this, else it will become a weapon of darkness, enmity and division.[8]

The Believer's Battle Cry: Pray!

Finally, Paul added one last element, one that reminds us that we do battle in God's strength, not our own:

> With all prayer and petition pray at all times in the Spirit, and with this in view, be on the alert with all perseverance and petition for all the saints. (Eph. 6:18)

Prayer, above all, expresses our reliance on God. We really are dependent on Him in all situations and at all times, as Paul's descriptions testify:

- *"With all prayer and petition"*: Our Enemy studies our weaknesses and plots his attacks accordingly, so we need to be just as precise in the requests we take to the Father on behalf of our fellow soldiers.

- *"Pray at all times in the Spirit"*: We need the Spirit's help to know how to pray and sometimes to have the strength to continue

---

7. Gerhard Kittel and Gerhard Friedrich, eds., *Theological Dictionary of the New Testament*, translated and abridged in one volume by Geoffrey W. Bromiley (1985; reprint, Grand Rapids, Mich.: William B. Eerdmans Publishing Co., 1992), p. 512.

8. Turner, "Ephesians," p. 1244.

praying (see John 16:13; Rom. 8:26). And we mustn't limit our prayer time to certain times of the day; our prayers need to be constant because our Adversary's attacks are relentless.

- *"Be on the alert with all perseverance"*: We need to pay attention, have our eyes trained to detect oncoming assaults. And no matter what, we have to keep on praying, not becoming discouraged if victory takes longer than we ever thought it would.

- *"For all the saints"*: We're all targets of Satan's fiery arrows, from the most mature to baby believers. No one outgrows the need for protection that a united defense in Christ provides.

Even the apostle Paul needed the prayerful safekeeping and encouragement of others:

> And pray on my behalf, that utterance may be given to me in the opening of my mouth, to make known with boldness the mystery of the gospel, for which I am an ambassador in chains; that in proclaiming it I may speak boldly, as I ought to speak. (Eph. 6:19–20)

"An ambassador in chains"—what a poignant description of the visible evidence of Satan's warfare against Christ and His people. We usually assume that Paul was fearless, impervious to discouragement, a man who let nothing stop him. Most of us probably see him as a "super-Christian" who was able to overcome opposition in a single bound! Who would have thought that he got scared too? That the words of truth sometimes got stuck in his fear-tightened throat?

But he was human, just like us, and humble and honest enough to admit his need and ask for help. For he knew that the Ephesians wouldn't be upholding him only. They would be furthering the ministry of Christ and His gospel's mystery—the mystery that plants the flag of God's grace in the midst of human misery, that brings the dead to life, and that reconciles the estranged under the shelter of Christ's cross.

✦ *Living Insights*

Christopher Lamb points out how ridiculous our armaments must appear to the world—but how truly effective they are:

> To the unbeliever [Paul's] equipment list might seem

like a useless jumble of religious ideas. Stalin asked, "How many divisions [of soldiers] has the Pope?" But the modern world has proved over and over again that the power of faith in God combined with unflinching moral courage and integrity can overturn the most immovable dictatorships and profoundly unjust governments.[9]

In the face of this world's evil—wars waged and lives extinguished for the sake of pride and greed, whole nations impoverished and starved because of a leader's voracious appetite for power, children exploited and degraded by those who make an idol of sexual pleasure—our only help comes from

> the confidence which the power of God can give. Through this people of faith know that because they desire only God's peace and justice, their cause cannot in the end be defeated. Truth holds them together, their peace with God keeps them stable, faith protects them from despair, and knowing God's plan of rescue keeps alive their hope. Their only weapons are the words of truth and love, fresh and sharp and healing.[10]

Have you put on God's full armor? How prepared are you to stand strong for His cause? Think through the pieces of armor Paul listed, and evaluate the state of your readiness.

Belt of truth. How well are you living the truth of God's Word? Are there any areas of your life where your integrity needs to be tightened up a notch?

_____

_____

_____

_____

_____

9. Christopher Lamb, "The Message of Ephesians," in *The Bible for Everyday Life*, ed. George Carey and Robin Keeley (Grand Rapids, Mich.: William B. Eerdmans Publishing Co., 1996), p. 251.

10. Lamb, "The Message of Ephesians," p. 251.

Breastplate of righteousness. How have you grown in the righteousness Christ secured for you? In what ways do your personal morality and holiness need to be reinforced?

_____

_____

_____

_____

_____

Boots of peace. Do you have trouble resting in the peace Christ has secured for you? Do you know why? How might Satan be assaulting you in this area?

_____

_____

_____

_____

_____

Shield of faith. What happens when troubles come your way? Do you tend to let go of God and panic? Or are you learning to hold fast to Him and the promises He has made? How is Satan challenging you in this area, and how sure is your defense?

_____

_____

_____

_____

_____

Helmet of salvation. How often do you remind yourself of your heavenly hope? Do you tend to get bogged down in the trenches of this earthly battle, forgetting that Christ has secured a very real victory?

_____

_____

_____

_____

_____

Sword of the Spirit. How sharp and polished is your knowledge of Scripture? Of the doctrines of our faith? Of the theological themes that give you the bigger picture of God's heart and plans? What can (and will) you do to strengthen yourself in this area? (The Books for Probing Further section at the end of this guide can give you some guidance.)

_____

_____

_____

_____

Prayer. How seriously do you take prayer? How much time do you commit to it? What would you like your prayer life to look like?

_____

_____

_____

_____

Spend some time in prayer right now, asking God to help you put on the armor He has provided. And intercede for those you know who are struggling in the thick of battle.

Chapter 26

HERE'S HOW TO
FINISH WELL
Ephesians 6:18–24

W e've certainly covered a lot of ground in Ephesians, haven't we? Paul has taken us from the "heavenly places" in chapter 1 to earth's spiritual battleground in chapter 6. In between, the apostle has shown us how the Lord:

- lavished His love and grace on us in redemption,

- took the alienated and made them cherished members of His own family,

- turned our scarring divisions into His healing unity,

- rescued us from the pit of deception and placed us on the pinnacle of truth,

- led us out of darkness to walk in His radiant light.

With reverence and excitement, Paul has revealed that, from our most intimate relationships to our work in the world, Jesus reigns over all in grace, peace, and love!

In fact, Paul's opening words spoke of grace and peace, remember (1:2)? And so do his closing thoughts. In reverse order, Paul bracketed all the glorious truths about what God has done for us and how we're to live them out with the Lord's peace, love, and grace (6:23–24).

As we join Paul once more, let's see if we can gain a few more insights into what it takes to become a people of God's peaceful, loving grace.

Stay Strong in Prayer

As we saw in our previous chapter, Paul counted on the power of prayer to uphold all of Christ's people—including himself:

> With all prayer and petition pray at all times in the Spirit, and with this in view, be on the alert with all perseverance and petition for all the saints,

206

and pray on my behalf, that utterance may be given
to me in the opening of my mouth. (vv. 18–19a)

Some commentators believe that prayer is another piece of our
spiritual armor, which is possible; but certainly it's one of the ways
we stand firm in the protection God has provided for us. We can
even think of prayer as the way we put our armor on.

And notice, Paul didn't set any age limit on who could wield
our spiritual weaponry in prayer. Little children can intercede for
others, taking their tender hearts to God, and so can men and
women in their eighties, nineties, and even hundreds! *All* of us are
a vital part of Christ's body; no one is unimportant or unneeded.
Prayer is something we can all do to help each other.

Aside from the answers we receive to our prayers, the act of
praying itself benefits us in many ways. It keeps us engaged in what's
happening around us. It focuses our time and energy on what God
is doing. It helps stabilize us when we're tempted to worry. And it
transforms us from negative people to positive believers, because it
turns our fear to hope.

Paul wanted the Ephesians to involve themselves in God's plan
for his life, specifically asking them to pray that when he opened
his mouth, God's words would come out (v. 19a). Remarkably, he
didn't pray to be released from his house arrest or for God to take
vengeance on his enemies. He simply wanted his "tongue [to be]
the pen of a ready writer," because his "heart overflow[ed] with a
good theme" (Ps. 45:1). And he also wanted the courage to proclaim
his theme—the gospel of God's grace in Jesus Christ.

Be Bold in Courage

And pray on my behalf, that utterance may be given
to me in the opening of my mouth, to make known
with boldness the mystery of the gospel, for which I
am an ambassador in chains; that in proclaiming it I
may speak boldly, as I ought to speak. (Eph. 6:19–20)

Yes, even Paul got intimidated and discouraged—he had been
beaten and stoned, and he knew what the Roman powers could do
to him. But he didn't want to live in fear. Instead, as he stood before
the greatest leaders of the world, he wanted to keep Christ preem-
inent and make His message known. He was, in effect, promoting
the sovereignty of one kingdom to the leaders of another. So he

asked the Ephesians to help shore up his courage to represent the true King as he should.

It's hard to speak openly and freely of Christ in a world that's hostile to Him, isn't it? Some of our fellow Christians have their homes and churches burned down, and some are beaten or raped, unjustly jailed, tortured, and murdered. Others of us feel stripped of our voice; we're ridiculed, mocked, and censored. All of us, no matter our situation, need the courage to stand by Christ and keep telling the truth. Souls are at stake—even if they are the souls of our enemies. And what we have to look forward to in heaven far outweighs the hurts this world can inflict (see 2 Cor. 4:17).

If you tend to be a fearful person, make Paul's prayer your own. And remember what Moses told the Israelites as they prepared to take the Promised Land for God:

> "Be strong and courageous, do not be afraid or trem-
> ble at them, for the Lord your God is the one who
> goes with you. He will not fail you or forsake you."
> (Deut. 31:6)

Cultivate Closeness with Faithful Friends

> But that you also may know about my circum-
> stances, how I am doing, Tychicus, the beloved
> brother and faithful minister in the Lord, will make
> everything known to you. I have sent him to you
> for this very purpose, so that you may know about us,
> and that he may comfort your hearts. (Eph. 6:21–22)

One look at the New Testament shows that Paul was a great letter-writer, since he wrote thirteen of its twenty-seven books! Not only did he diligently convey Christ's gospel to people in widespread regions, but he also kept in touch with those he'd ministered to over the years. His relationships weren't merely mentoring ones; he had dear friends on whom he relied for both encouragement and help. And Tychicus was such a friend.

"Beloved" and "faithful," Tychicus would bring Paul's personal touch to the Ephesians. He would tell them how well Paul was holding up under his arrest and how the saving word of the gospel was spreading even further through Paul's imprisonment. How did he know these things? From Paul himself, who didn't approach his ministry as a one-man show but went to great lengths to establish and maintain friendships. Just take a look at the end of many of his letters to see how many friends he had (see Rom. 16; 1 Cor. 16:19; Col. 4:7–15; 2 Tim. 4:19–21; and Philemon)!

God has designed us to live in community—to refresh others and be refreshed, to encourage others and be encouraged, to care for others and be cared for, to give empathy and receive it, to love and be loved. We're not called to a Lone Ranger life (even he had his friend Tonto!). Do you have friends you can turn to for encouragement, help, and sheer enjoyment? Or are you afraid of imposing on others or bothering them? No matter what our age, something inside us starts to wither without the rich soil of friendship.

So take a tip from Paul—let others into your life so that they may know what God is doing in and through you, and open the windows of your heart so that Christ can make Himself more deeply known to you through your friends' love and care.

Let Love for Christ Abound

As he so beautifully began his letter, so Paul eloquently closed it in a similar way:

> Peace be to the brethren, and love with faith, from God the Father and the Lord Jesus Christ. Grace be with all those who love our Lord Jesus Christ with incorruptible love. (Eph. 6:23–24)

Let's slow down and take in all that Paul said here.

Peace to God's Family

"Peace," Paul said, for Christ "Himself is our peace, who . . . broke down the barrier of the dividing wall . . . so that in Himself He might make the two into one new man, thus establishing peace" (2:14–15). With Christ having established peace with God and between people, those called by His name are to live out that peace, "being diligent to preserve the unity of the Spirit in the bond of peace" (4:3). This peaceful way of life was first on Paul's mind, and close behind it was love, because he knew it was the best means of achieving peace.

Add Love to Your Faith

"Have love in addition to your faith," Paul next told them,[1] knowing that all the doctrinal precision in the world meant nothing without love for Christ and love for each other bringing it to life (see 1 Cor. 13:1–3). How many times had Paul reminded the Ephesians (and us) of God's love?

- "In love He predestined us to adoption as sons through Jesus Christ" (Eph. 1:4b–5a).

- "But God . . . because of His great love with which He loved us . . . made us alive together with Christ" (2:4–5).

- "That you, being rooted and grounded in love, may be able to comprehend with all the saints what is the breadth and length and height and depth, and to know the love of Christ which surpasses knowledge" (3:17b–19a).

The church is supposed to be the community that shows the world what it's supposed to be. And the way we do this is through love (see John 13:34–35). Christ is the Vine of love, we are the branches growing out from love, and we're meant to bear the fruit of love (see John 15:1–11). As Paul told us, we're to:

- bear with one another in love (Eph. 4:2)

- speak the truth to one another in love (v. 15)

- build up each other and, consequently, Christ's whole body in love (v. 16)

- walk in love, just as Christ has loved each of us (5:2)

- love our spouses with Christ's self-giving love (vv. 25, 28, 33)

- love Christ with a deathless love (6:24)

Paul used the word *love* fifteen times in fourteen verses in this letter. But, sadly, the Ephesians seemed to pass down everything to the next generation but this. About thirty-five years later, Christ Himself, through the apostle John, had this to say to the church at Ephesus:

---

1. See Charles Hodge, *Commentary on the Epistle to the Ephesians* (1857; reprint, Grand Rapids, Mich.: William B. Eerdmans Publishing Co., 1994), p. 396; and John R. W. Stott, *The Message of Ephesians: God's New Society*, The Bible Speaks Today Series (Downers Grove, Ill.: InterVarsity Press, 1979), p. 290.

"'I know your deeds and your toil and perseverance, and that you cannot tolerate evil men, and
you put to the test those who call themselves apostles, and they are not, and you found them to be
false; and you have perseverance and have endured
for My name's sake, and have not grown weary. But
I have this against you, *that you have left your first
love.*'" (Rev. 2:2–4, emphasis added)

As we go forward with Paul's letter in our minds, let's not make
the same mistake the Ephesians made. Let's remember to take it in
our hearts as well.

Grace Rests on All Who Love Christ

"Grace is God's gift to you," Paul urged us to remember (see
Eph. 2:8). His grace, given freely and lavishly out of the storehouse
of His immense riches, brings us redemption, forgiveness, new life,
salvation, and spiritual gifts (1:6–7; 2:5, 7–8; 4:7). Why would God
do this for us? "So that in the ages to come He might show the surpassing riches of His grace in kindness toward us in Christ Jesus" (2:7).

God delights to lavish kindness on us—but notice, this grace
comes only through Christ, only to those who trust Him as their
Savior and welcome Him into their hearts forever.[2] In a life lived
in God's grace, we don't boast of ourselves; rather, we boast of the
incredible, magnificent, surpassing love of God the Father, His Son
Jesus Christ, and their Holy Spirit.

Are you ready to let God's living word in Ephesians change you
forever? If you start now, you can be assured that the Spirit will do
everything in His power to help you finish well. Then you can say
with Paul:

I have fought the good fight, I have finished the

---

2. A. Skevington Wood and John Stott provide a slightly different interpretation of this
verse. They propose that the phrase "incorruptible love" goes with God's grace instead of
believers' love. In this sense, Paul would have been saying that "all those who love our Lord
Jesus Christ" will know God's grace forever in eternity, where "the corruptible [literally] must
put on the incorruptible [literally], and this mortal must put on immortality" (1 Cor. 15:53).
With this rendering, Ephesians would have begun with us peering into eternity past and
closed with us looking ahead to eternity future. See Wood, "Ephesians," in *The Expositor's
Bible Commentary*, gen. ed. Frank E. Gaebelein (Grand Rapids, Mich.: Zondervan Publishing
House, Regency Reference Library, 1978), vol. 11, p. 92; and Stott, *The Message of Ephesians*,
pp. 290–91.

course, I have kept the faith; in the future there is laid up for me the crown of righteousness, which the Lord, the righteous Judge, will award to me on that day; and not only to me, but also to all who have loved His appearing. (2 Tim. 4:7–8)

May the Lord's peace, love, and grace be with you always!

🕸 *Living Insights*

Well, we've reached the end of this study on Paul's letter to the Ephesians, but we can never reach the end of its impact! Like a beautiful piece of music that plays on in our minds and lifts our spirits, the golden notes of Paul's composition linger in our souls and lift our hearts to God.

What truths and insights are reverberating in your spirit? Take some time now to do a little reflecting.

What did you learn about God that you didn't know before or maybe hadn't truly realized?

_____

_____

_____

_____

_____

How about what God in Christ has done for you? What insights did you discover, especially from chapters 1 and 2?

_____

_____

_____

_____

_____

How has Paul's teaching on God's grace, love, and peace impacted you?

_____

_____

_____

_____

_____

_____

What have you learned about Christian ethics through studying this letter? What difference has it made in your life?

_____

_____

_____

_____

_____

_____

How has Paul's picture of life without Christ affected you? For example, has it softened your heart toward nonbelievers? Has it encouraged you to stay truer to Christ so that His light can shine unobstructed into this darkened world? Or something else?

_____

_____

_____

_____

_____

Have any of your relationships changed as a result of Paul's teaching? If so, how?

_____

_____

_____

_____

_____

_____

Do you feel more committed to preserving our unity in Christ? In what ways can you work toward this and help others see its value?

_____

_____

_____

_____

_____

_____

Did you need to *unlearn* anything—did Paul correct your thinking in any areas? If so, what are they? What did you have to relearn?

_____

_____

_____

_____

_____

_____

What do you think is Satan's most-used strategy in your life, your family's life, your church's life, and in your society? What one thing would you pray for in each of these areas?

_____

_____

_____

_____

_____

_____

What touched you most deeply in this letter? How do you plan to make this more a part of your life?

_____

_____

_____

_____

As you prepare to take all that you've learned into your world, may you carry Paul's prayers, and ours, with you:

> *May God our Father give you a spiritual mind so that you may know Him more completely. May He enlighten your heart's eyes to see the certainty of your hope, the glorious riches of your inheritance, and the incalculable power the Lord exerts on your behalf!*
>
> *May His Spirit strengthen you, may Christ make His home in you, and may His love take root and blossom fully in your life!*
>
> *Now to the Lord who does more good for us than we could ever imagine or dream—to Him be the glory! May His church glorify Him through His wonderful Son in all places and in all ages to the very edges of eternity!*
> (adapted from Eph. 1:17–19a; 3:16–21)

BOOKS FOR PROBING FURTHER

To learn more about Paul's letter to the Ephesians and the life of unity, grace, and love Christ has called us to, we recommend the following resources.

Commentaries

Barclay, William. *The Letters to the Galatians and Ephesians*. Rev. ed. The Daily Study Bible Series. Philadelphia, Pa.: Westminster Press, 1976.

Barton, Bruce B., and Philip Comfort, Kent Keller, Linda K. Taylor, and Dave Veerman. *Ephesians*. Life Application Bible Commentary Series. Wheaton, Ill.: Tyndale House Publishers, 1996.

Boice, James Montgomery. *Ephesians: An Expositional Commentary*. Grand Rapids, Mich.: Baker Books, 1997.

Hodge, Charles. *Commentary on the Epistle to the Ephesians*. 1857. Reprint, Grand Rapids, Mich.: William B. Eerdmans Publishing Co., 1994.

Hughes, R. Kent. *Ephesians: The Mystery of the Body of Christ*. Preaching the Word Series. Wheaton, Ill.: Good News Publishers, Crossway Books, 1990.

Stott, John R. W. *The Message of Ephesians: God's New Society*. The Bible Speaks Today Series. Downers Grove, Ill.: InterVarsity Press, 1979.

Turner, Max. "Ephesians." In *New Bible Commentary: 21st Century Edition*. 4th ed., rev. Gen. ed. D. A. Carson, R. T. France, J. A. Motyer, and G. J. Wenham (Downers Grove, Ill.: InterVarsity Press, 1994.

Wiersbe, Warren W. *Be Rich: Are You Losing the Things That Money Can't Buy?* Wheaton, Ill.: Scripture Press Publications, Victor Books, 1976.

Topical Studies

Allender, Dan, and Tremper Longman III. *Intimate Allies: Rediscovering God's Design for Marriage and Becoming Soul Mates for Life.* Wheaton, Ill.: Tyndale House Publishers, 1995.

Briner, Bob. *Roaring Lambs: A Gentle Plan to Radically Change Our World.* Grand Rapids, Mich.: Zondervan Publishing House, 1993.

Colson, Charles, with Ellen Santilli Vaughn. *The Body: Being Light in the Darkness.* Dallas, Tex.: Word Publishing, 1992.

Crabb, Larry. *The Safest Place on Earth.* Dallas, Tex.: Word Books, 1999.

Gangel, Kenneth O. *Unwrap Your Spiritual Gifts.* Wheaton, Ill.: Scripture Press Publications, Victor Books, 1983.

Glaspey, Terry W. *Children of a Greater God: Awakening Your Child's Moral Imagination.* Eugene, Ore.: Harvest House Publishers, 1995.

Hall, Dudley. *Grace Works: Letting God Rescue You from Empty Religion.* Ann Arbor, Mich.: Servant Publications, Vine Books, 1992.

Lutzer, Erwin W. *All One Body—Why Don't We Agree?* Wheaton, Ill.: Tyndale House Publishers, 1989.

Malphurs, Aubrey. *Maximizing Your Effectiveness: How to Discover and Develop Your Divine Design.* Grand Rapids, Mich.: Baker Books, 1995.

Miller, Calvin. *Disarming the Darkness: A Guide to Spiritual Warfare.* Grand Rapids, Mich.: Zondervan Publishing House, 1998.

Perkins, Spencer, and Chris Rice. *More Than Equals: Racial Healing for the Sake of the Gospel.* Downers Grove, Ill.: InterVarsity Press, 1993.

Plantinga, Cornelius, Jr. *Not the Way It's Supposed to Be: A Breviary of Sin.* Grand Rapids, Mich.: William B. Eerdmans Publishing Co., 1995.

Sherman, Doug, and William Hendricks. *Your Work Matters to God.* Colorado Springs, Colo.: NavPress, 1987.

Stedman, Ray C. *Body Life.* 3d ed. Ventura, Calif.: Gospel Light Publications, Regal Books, 1979.

Yancey, Philip. *What's So Amazing about Grace?* Grand Rapids, Mich.: Zondervan Publishing House, 1997.

Some of the books listed may be out of print and available only through a library. For those currently available, please contact your local Christian bookstore. Books by Charles R. Swindoll may be obtained through the Insight for Living Resource Center, as well as many books by other authors. Just call the IFL office that serves you.

Insight for Living also has Bible study guides available on many books of the Bible as well as on a variety of topics, Bible characters, and contemporary issues. For more information, see the ordering instructions that follow and contact the office that serves you.

Ordering Information

Becoming a People of Grace

If you would like to order additional Bible study guides, purchase the audiocassette series that accompanies this guide, or request our product catalogs, please contact the office that serves you.

United States and International locations:

Insight for Living
Post Office Box 269000
Plano, TX 75026-9000

1-800-772-8888, 24 hours a day, seven days a week (U.S. contacts)
International constituents may contact the U.S. office through mail queries.

Canada:

Insight for Living Ministries
Post Office Box 2510
Vancouver, BC, Canada V6B 3W7

1-800-663-7639, 24 hours a day, seven days a week
infocanada@insight.org

Australia:

Insight for Living, Inc.
20 Albert Street
Blackburn, VIC 3130, Australia

Toll-free 1800 772 888 or (03) 9877-4277, 8:30 A.M. to 5:00 P.M., Monday to Friday
iflaus@insight.org

World Wide Web:

www.insight.org

Bible Study Guide Subscription Program

Bible study guide subscriptions are available. Please call or write the office nearest you to find out how you can receive our Bible study guides on a regular basis.